24 Hour Telephone Renewals 0845 071 4343
HARINGEY LIBRARIES
THIS BOOK MUST BE RETURNED ON OR BEFORE
THE LAST DATE MARKED BELOW

To

Online renewals – visit libraries.haringey.gov.uk

published by Haringey Council's Communications Unit 973.16 • 08/12

70001617783 9

PRE-INTERMEDIATE LEVEL

Founding Editor: John Milne

The Macmillan Readers provide a choice of enjoyable reading material for learners of English. The series is published at six levels—Starter, Beginner, Elementary, Pre-intermediate, Intermediate and Upper.

Level Control
Information, structure and vocabulary are controlled to suit the students' ability at each level.

The number of words at each level:

Starter	about 300 basic words
Beginner	about 600 basic words
Elementary	about 1100 basic words
Pre-intermediate	about 1400 basic words
Intermediate	about 1600 basic words
Upper	about 2200 basic words

Vocabulary
Some difficult words and phrases in this book are important for understanding the story. Some of these words are explained in the story, some are shown in the pictures, and others are marked with a number like this: ...³. Words with a number are explained in the Glossary.

Answer Keys
Answer Keys for the *Points for Understanding* and the *Exercises* sections can be found at www.macmillanenglish.com.

Contents

A Note About the Author		*4*
A Note About This Story		*6*
The People in This Story		*7*
1	Vevey	*11*
2	Mrs Costello	*24*
3	The Château de Chillon	*36*
4	Rome	*41*
5	Mrs Walker Turns Her Back on Daisy Miller	*57*
6	Daisy Miller Goes Too Far	*63*
7	Winterbourne Makes a Decision	*69*
	Points for Understanding	*77*
	Glossary	*80*
	Exercises	*87*

A Note About the Author

Henry James was born on April 15th, 1843, in New York City. His parents were rich, intelligent and well-educated. His father was interested in religion and literature.

When he was a young boy, Henry James traveled with his family between America and Europe many times. He was educated by tutors[1] in Geneva, London and Paris. He enjoyed reading literature from Britain, France, Germany, Russia and Italy, in English.

When he was nineteen, James attended Harvard Law School. But soon he knew that he did not want to be a lawyer. He wanted to read and write books. In 1864, his first short story, A *Tragedy of Error*, was published. From this time until his death, James worked very hard. He wrote novels, essays, short stories, travel books and biographies. He also wrote excellent reviews[2] about art and artists, literature and authors, plays and playwrights.

James lived in Paris for a year in 1875. While he was there, he met the writers Gustave Flaubert and Ivan Turgenev. However, in 1876, he decided to make his home in England. He lived in an apartment in London for a year. Then in 1897, he moved to Rye, a small town in the southern county[3] of Sussex. He visited America again several times, but he lived at Lamb House in Rye for the rest of his life.

When the First World War started in 1915, James was shocked. He was also angry that America would not fight with the British in the war, so he became a British citizen[4]. James never married. He enjoyed meeting interesting and intelligent people and he was a popular guest. During the winter of 1878–9 he received 107 dinner invitations! The writers Edith Wharton, H. G. Wells and Gustave Flaubert became his friends. James admired[5] the work of writers Nathaniel Hawthorne, Honoré de Balzac and Ivan Turgenev.

Henry James wrote 22 books, 12 plays, and 112 short stories, as well as a great number of non-fiction books and magazine articles. Many of Henry James' stories have been made into movies.

People who study the work of Henry James often divide his writing career[6] into three parts.

In the first part, James' novels describe American visitors in Europe. Europe's culture and polite society[7] was older than America's, and Europeans behaved in a more formal[8] way. Examples of the these stories are: *Roderick Hudson* (1875), *The American* (1877), *Daisy Miller* (1878), *Washington Square* (1880), *Portrait of a Lady* (1881), *The Bostonians* (1886), *Princess Casamassima* (1886), and *The Aspern Papers* (1888).

In the second part of his career, James wrote novels about politics and women in society. Examples are: *The Tragic Muse* (1890), *The Spoils of Poynton* (1897), *What Maisie Knew* (1897), *In the Cage* (1898) and *The Awkward Age* (1899).

In the third part of his writing career, James studied the psychology[9] of his British and American characters in his novels. Some of the books of this period are: *The Wings of a Dove* (1902), *The Ambassadors* (1903), and *The Golden Bowl* (1904). Many people think that *The Ambassadors* is James' finest novel.

Henry James was given the British honor[10] of the Order of Merit. He died on February 28th, 1916. He was seventy-two years old.

A Note About This Story

This story starts in 1875. Daisy Miller, a young American girl, does not understand why her behavior makes people angry and upset. Daisy likes to have fun. She does not realize that she is behaving incorrectly and her mother does not help her. The author shows the difference between the members of polite society and people who have only recently become rich.

Members of polite society had owned land, money and property for many hundreds of years. Their families were rich and powerful. They had many servants and did not have to work. In the eighteenth and nineteenth centuries, rich people often traveled through Europe. They watched plays and listened to concerts. They attended dinner parties and dances. They visited art galleries to look at paintings, and they admired old buildings and beautiful views.

Good manners—the correct way that people behaved and spoke—were very important. Well-educated people with good manners spoke quietly and intelligently. They thought about other peoples' feelings and they made sure that they did not upset them. In polite society, women did not travel alone, or visit places alone. A woman must not be alone with a man who was not her relative. Young women had to be introduced to young men whom they did not know. These were the rules of correct behavior in polite society.

In this novel, the author shows how a pretty young American breaks the rules of society. Daisy flirts[11] with the men that she meets and she often spends time[12] alone with them. She does not know why this is wrong. The Millers have a lot of money, and they have not been educated in a formal, European way. The rich, older people in the story are shocked by Daisy's behavior and they turn away from the Millers.

The People in This Story

Frederick Winterbourne

Daisy Miller
Randolph Miller

Mrs Costello

Mrs Walker

Mrs Miller   Eugenio

Giovanelli

DAISY MILLER

The Trois Couronnes hotel is very popular with Americans.

1

Vevey

The little town of Vevey, in Switzerland, stands beside Lake Geneva. Many travelers come to visit the beautiful blue lake, and so its shore[13] is crowded with[14] hotels. There are many different kinds of hotel around the lake. There are new, grand hotels which are painted white. And there are also small *pensions*—simple, old hotels with just a few rooms. The grand hotels have lots of rooms with big windows, and flags fly on their roofs. The *pensions* are smaller, with fewer rooms. However, one of the hotels in Vevey is very different from the others because it is old but also very comfortable. This hotel is named the *Trois Couronnes*—the Three Crowns[15].

The hotel is very popular with Americans. Many American travelers visit Vevey in summer and a lot of them stay at the Trois Couronnes. At this time, the town is full of fashionable[16] young girls in beautiful dresses. At night in the hotel, you can hear the sounds of excited voices and lively music. The voices have American accents[17] and an orchestra plays dance music. You can almost believe that you are in America! However, the Trois Couronnes is a European hotel. It has neatly-dressed[18] German waiters. And in the garden you might meet a Russian princess, or the son of a Polish gentleman.

There is a wonderful view from the hotel. From its big windows, you can see the top of the Dent du Midi—a tall, snow-covered mountain. And you can also see the towers[19] of the Château de Chillon, an old castle which stands beside the lake. All these things remind you that you are in Switzerland, not America.

One beautiful morning in June, a young American gentleman sat in the garden of the Trois Couronnes. He was enjoying the view across the lake. His name was Frederick Winterbourne, and the day before, he had arrived in Vevey from his home in Geneva. Winterbourne had come to visit his aunt, who was staying in Vevey for the summer. Winterbourne was twenty-seven years old, and he had lived in Geneva for many years. He had plenty of money and did not have to work. Winterbourne's friends said that he spent his time studying. But they did not know what he was studying, or where! Other people said that Winterbourne was in love with an older, foreign lady, who lived in Geneva. They said that was why he stayed in the city.

A week earlier, Winterbourne's aunt—Mrs Costello—had come to the Trois Couronnes. She had asked her nephew to visit her there. But early this morning, she had sent Winterbourne a message. She was not well. She had a headache—she almost always had a headache—and she could not see him. So Winterbourne had walked around the town, and then he had eaten his breakfast at the hotel. He was now sitting in the garden of the hotel, drinking coffee.

Winterbourne had just finished his cup of coffee when a small boy came walking along the path. The boy was about nine or ten years old and had a pale face. He was wearing short trousers, with long, red, woolen stockings and he was carrying a long stick. As he walked, the boy pushed the stick at anything he saw—flowers, chairs, even the edges of the ladies' long dresses. When he came near to Winterbourne, the boy stopped. He looked at the coffee tray on the table in front of Winterbourne.

"May I have some sugar?" he asked. He spoke English with an American accent.

Winterbourne looked at the tray. There were several lumps[20] of sugar in a bowl.

"May I have some sugar?" he asked.

"Yes, you may have some sugar," he replied. "But I don't think that it's very good for little boys."

The boy put two sugar lumps in his pocket, and a third lump into his mouth.

"It's very hard," he said.

"Don't hurt your teeth," said Winterbourne kindly.

"I haven't got many teeth," replied the boy. "Most of them have come out. I've only got seven teeth left. My mother counted them last night, and another one came out immediately afterward. She'll be mad with me[21] if any more come out. It's not my fault[22]. The European weather makes my teeth fall out. They didn't come out in America."

Winterbourne laughed. "Your mother will certainly be mad with you, if you eat all that sugar."

"I'm eating the sugar because I don't have any candy[23]," replied the boy. "I can't get American candy here. American candy is the best candy."

Then he put one leg over the walking stick and ran up and down the path, as if he was riding a horse.

"And are American boys the best boys?" asked Winterbourne, when the boy stopped in front of him.

"I don't know. I'm an American boy," said the child.

"And I can see that you are *one* of the best!" replied Winterbourne, laughing.

The boy looked at Winterbourne. "Are you an American man?" he asked.

"Yes, I am," Winterbourne replied.

"American men are the best," said the boy.

Winterbourne watched the boy eating another lump of sugar. He had first come to Europe when he was about nine years old too. "Was I as lively as this boy?" he thought.

"Here's my sister," said the boy suddenly. "She's an American girl."

Winterbourne looked along the path. He saw a young

lady walking toward them.

"American girls are the best girls," he said to the boy.

"My sister isn't the best," said the child. "She's always getting mad with me."

"Maybe she gets mad with you because you do bad things," said Winterbourne.

The young lady had now come closer. She was wearing a white dress that was decorated with frills and ribbons[24]. And she was holding a parasol[25]. She was very pretty. She stopped in front of Winterbourne. The boy was now using the stick to jump across the path. He pushed one end of the walking stick into the ground and jumped, again and again.

"Randolph," said the young lady, "*what* are you doing?"

"I'm climbing mountains," replied Randolph. He turned toward Winterbourne and nodded his head. "He's an American man!" he said suddenly.

Winterbourne was not sure what to do. He stood up. Young men did not speak to young unmarried ladies who they did not know. It was not correct behavior. But the boy *had* almost introduced him. And when a pretty young American girl stands in front of you in a hotel garden, it is difficult to do nothing. So Winterbourne decided to speak to her. He bowed[26].

"This young man and I have just met each other," he said, very politely.

The American girl looked quickly at Winterbourne. Then she turned away, and looked across the lake at the mountains.

"Have I been too bold[27]?" Winterbourne thought. "We haven't been introduced. Maybe I shouldn't have spoken to her." But it was too late to stop the conversation now. While he was thinking of something more to say, the young lady spoke to the boy again.

"I hope that you aren't going to take that stick to Italy!" she said.

She was wearing a white dress that was decorated with frills and ribbons. And she was holding a parasol.

"Are you going to Italy?" asked Winterbourne, politely.

"Yes, sir," she replied. She said nothing more, and Winterbourne felt embarrassed[28].

"Which way are you traveling to Italy?" he asked, after a moment.

"I don't know," said the young lady. "I expect that we're going over some mountain. Randolph, what mountain are we going over?"

"I don't know," said Randolph. "I don't want to go to Italy. I want to go to America."

"Oh, Italy is a beautiful place," said Winterbourne.

"Can you get candy there?" asked Randolph loudly.

"I hope not," said his sister. "I think that you've had enough candy. And Mother thinks so too."

"I haven't had any candy for a long time," replied the boy, jumping about. "I haven't had any for a hundred weeks."

The young lady looked down at her dress and touched the ribbons. Then she sat down on a chair beside the table.

Winterbourne felt a little bolder now. "It's a beautiful view," he said, pointing to the lake and the mountains.

He no longer felt embarrassed because he saw that the young lady was not embarrassed herself. It was unusual for a young gentleman to talk to a young lady in this way. However, she was not upset by his boldness. She often looked away from him when he spoke to her. Maybe this was the way that she usually behaved.

Winterbourne talked a little more. He pointed toward some of the places and things that they could see from the hotel garden.

The young lady looked at his face more often now, and without any embarrassment. Some people might have thought that her look was too bold. And they might have thought that she was not behaving correctly. But the young lady's expression[29] was honest and innocent[30].

"I've not seen such a pretty young lady for a very long time," Winterbourne said to himself. He loved all beautiful things and he enjoyed studying beauty. He looked at this young American girl very carefully. What could he learn about her by looking at her face? She had an interesting face, but it did not show her feelings. Her nose and mouth were small and pretty, and she had large bright eyes. But her face was not absolutely perfect—it was not truly beautiful.

"Maybe she's a flirt," Winterbourne thought.

The young lady soon showed that she enjoyed talking. She told Winterbourne that her home was in the state of New York. And she also told him that she was going to Rome for the winter, with her mother and Randolph.

Winterbourne wanted to find out more, so he put his hand on her brother's arm and pulled the boy toward him.

"What's your name?" he asked the child.

"Randolph C. Miller," said the boy. He pointed the stick at his sister. "And her name is Daisy Miller. But that isn't her real name. Her real name is Annie P. Miller. And my father's name is Ezra B. Miller. But he didn't come with us to Europe. He's in America. He's got a big business in Schenectady[31], and he's very rich."

"Randolph, you shouldn't say that!" said Miss Miller.

The little boy walked away, dragging his stick along the path.

"My brother doesn't like Europe," said Miss Miller. "He wants to go back."

"To Schenectady?" asked Winterbourne.

"Yes," she said. "He doesn't have any friends here. He has no-one to play with."

"Does your brother have a tutor?" asked Winterbourne.

"Mother was going to get him a tutor," Miss Miller replied. "We met an American lady named Mrs Sanders, and she told us about a very good tutor. We were going to ask *him*

18

to travel with us. But Randolph said that he didn't want a tutor traveling with us. Randolph is very smart[32]. He already knows lots of things, and he's going to attend college."

Miss Miller talked about her family, and about many other things. While she talked, she looked at the garden, at the people walking past, and at the view across the lake. She talked to Winterbourne as if she had known him for a long time. He liked this very much. He had not heard a young girl talk so much for many years. Miss Miller sat very quietly, but her lips and eyes moved all the time. She told Winterbourne about her family's travels in Europe, and she talked about the hotels where they had stayed.

"I've never seen so many hotels in my life," she said. "There are so many hotels here in Europe!" But Miss Miller was not complaining[33]. She seemed to be very pleased with everything. She thought that the hotels were all very good. And she thought that Europe was charming[34].

"I haven't been disappointed at all," she went on. "Maybe I'm not disappointed because I'd heard so much about Europe before. I have many friends who've been here many times. And, of course, I have so many dresses and things from Paris.

"The only thing that I don't like," she said, "is European society. There isn't any society here—no dinners, or parties or dances. Well, I think there's *some* society somewhere, but I haven't found it. I do like society, and I've always had a lot of it. I've been in society in Schenectady, and in New York. In New York City I had lots of society. Last winter, seventeen dinners were organized for me. Three of the dinners were organized by gentlemen.

"I've more friends in New York than in Schenectady," Daisy Miller continued. "I have more gentlemen friends in that city, and more young lady friends too." She stopped talking for a moment. Then she looked at Winterbourne with her bright eyes and smiled gently.

19

"I've always enjoyed the friendship of gentlemen," she said.

Winterbourne did not know what to say. Polite young ladies did not talk in this way. Miss Daisy Miller was very charming, but she was also very forward[35]. Was she just a pretty, innocent young girl from New York State? Or was she dishonest and too bold? Was she a person who always made sure that she got what she wanted?

"I've lived in Geneva for too long," Winterbourne thought. "I don't understand Americans anymore."

He had certainly never met a young girl like Daisy Miller before. Winterbourne decided that she was probably a flirt— a pretty American flirt. Daisy Miller certainly did not flirt because she wanted men's admiration. He had known some older, married women who behaved in this way. They were dangerous, terrible women. But Daisy was unsophisticated— she was not experienced in the ways of the world.

"Yes, she's just a pretty American flirt," Winterbourne said to himself. He was pleased that he now understood her. But he had never really known a flirt before, and he was not sure how to behave with one.

"Have you been to that old castle?" asked Daisy, pointing with her parasol at the Château de Chillon.

"Yes, several times," replied Winterbourne. "Have you been there too?"

"No, I haven't. I do want to visit it. I can't leave Vevey without seeing that old castle."

"It's a lovely place," said Winterbourne, "and it's easy to get there. There's a boat which takes visitors across the lake."

"Yes, we wanted to go to the castle last week, but my mother wasn't well. Perhaps we'll go this week, if Randolph will come," said Daisy.

"Your brother doesn't want to go?" asked Winterbourne.

"He says that he doesn't really like old castles," she

replied. "He wants to stay at the hotel. Mother doesn't want him to stay there alone, and our guide won't stay with him. So we haven't visited many places in Vevey. But we really must go there," she said, looking at the château again.

"Couldn't you ask someone to stay with Randolph one afternoon?" said Winterbourne.

Daisy looked at him. "I wish that you would stay with him!" she said gently.

Winterbourne was quiet for a moment. Then he suddenly said, "I'd prefer to go to Chillon with you."

"With me?" repeated Daisy, calmly[36].

Winterbourne knew that he had been very bold. If he had made a suggestion like this to any other young girl, she would have been shocked. Miss Miller seemed very calm, but he was not sure if she was offended[37]. So he said, very politely, "Your mother must come too, of course."

But Daisy Miller certainly did not think that Winterbourne had been too bold.

"I don't think that my mother would like to go," she said quickly. "She doesn't like to go out in the afternoons. But did you mean what you said? Would you really like to go to the castle?"

"Very much," said Winterbourne.

"Then let's arrange a visit," she said. "If mother will stay with Randolph, I'm sure that Eugenio will too."

"Who is Eugenio?" asked Winterbourne.

"Eugenio is our guide," Miss Miller replied. "He's a very good guide. But he's very neat and correct. And he doesn't like to stay with Randolph because he's such a lively little boy. But I'm sure that Eugenio will stay at the hotel with Randolph, if Mother is there. Then we can go to the castle."

Winterbourne could not believe what this young woman was saying. Miss Miller was making plans to spend the day alone with him—without her mother, brother, or the guide!

21

He was shocked, but he was pleased. He almost wanted to kiss Miss Miller's hand.

But at that moment, a tall, handsome man came toward them. He was wearing a long jacket and he had a fine gold watch-chain[38].

"Oh hello, Eugenio!" said Miss Miller, in a friendly voice.

The guide looked at Winterbourne, from his head to his feet. Then he turned to the young lady.

"Mademoiselle[39], lunch is ready," he said.

Daisy stood up slowly. "Eugenio," she said. "I'm going to visit that old castle."

"You're going to the Château de Chillon, mademoiselle?" asked the guide sharply. "You have made some plans?" His voice showed that he did not approve[40] of this idea. Young women in polite society should not behave this way. They should not be alone with young gentlemen.

"How rude this man is!" Winterbourne thought.

Suddenly, Daisy saw that Eugenio disapproved. She was embarrassed for a moment—but only for a moment. She turned toward Winterbourne.

"You will come, won't you?" she asked. "Do you promise?"

"I promise!" he replied.

"Are you staying in this hotel?" she said. "And are you really an American?"

Eugenio was looking at Winterbourne. The expression in the guide's eyes was proud and angry.

"This man thinks that Miss Miller tries to meet strangers," Winterbourne said to himself. "She often looks for gentlemen to meet. That is what he thinks. And he believes that she is too friendly with these new friends."

"Miss Miller, I shall introduce you to my aunt," Winterbourne said. "She'll tell you all about me."

"And then we shall soon go to the Château de Chillon," said Miss Miller.

A tall, handsome man came toward them.

She smiled, lifted her parasol above her head, and walked back to the hotel with Eugenio.

Winterbourne watched Daisy Miller as she walked along the path. The edge of her long white dress moved slowly along the ground behind her.

"She walks like a princess," Winterbourne thought, as she disappeared inside the hotel.

2

Mrs Costello

As soon as his aunt was feeling better, Winterbourne went to visit her. His aunt, Mrs Costello, was a widow—her husband had died many years ago. She had a lot of money, and she was an important lady in society. However, she was often unwell—she had headaches. "If I didn't have so many headaches, I would have done a lot of great things in the world," Mrs Costello often said.

Everyone noticed Mrs Costello. She had a long pale face and a high nose. She had lots of bright white hair, which was curled on the top of her head. And she looked important.

Mrs Costello had not seen Winterbourne for many years, and she was very pleased with him. She told him how she had become an important person in New York society.

"Of course, I only meet with the *right* people and go to the *best* dinners and parties," Mrs Costello said.

Winterbourne's aunt described New York society to her nephew. She said that each person had a different place in society. In the city of New York, everyone was either more or less important than somebody else.

She told him how she had become an important person in New York society.

Winterbourne asked Mrs Costello about the Millers. He had promised to introduce Daisy to his aunt.

"Have you seen an American family, here in the hotel?" he said. "There's a mother, a daughter and a little boy."

"And they have a guide?" said Mrs Costello. "Oh yes, I've seen them. I've seen them, heard them, and tried to stay away from them."

Mrs Costello did not think that the Millers were from the best society.

"You don't approve of them?" Winterbourne said.

"They are very common[41]," said Mrs Costello. "They are not the right sort of people."

"The young girl is very pretty," said Winterbourne.

"Yes, she *is* pretty," replied his aunt. "But she's also very common."

"Yes, maybe you are right," said Winterbourne, after a few moments.

"Miss Miller looks charming, of course," continued Mrs Costello. "And she wears beautiful clothes. But she's much too friendly with her mother's guide. She and her mother behave as if he's their friend. They behave as if that guide is a gentleman. He sits with them in the garden in the evening. Maybe he eats dinner with them! The Millers shouldn't make friends with someone who works for them. It just isn't correct behavior."

Winterbourne listened carefully to his aunt. The things that she said helped him to decide about Daisy. She certainly behaved in a wild and informal way.

"Well, *I'm* not a guide, but she was very charming to me," he said.

"You've already met her?" said Mrs Costello. "Why didn't you tell me this?"

"We just met in the garden, and we talked a little," Winterbourne replied.

"You met in the garden! And what did you say?" she asked.

"I told Miss Miller that I would introduce her to you," he replied. "She's a very nice girl."

"I don't think that you really believe that," said Mrs Costello.

"She's very unsophisticated," Winterbourne said. "But she's very pretty, and I think she's very nice. In fact, I'm going to take her to the Château de Chillon."

"You and Miss Miller are going there together? But you've only been here for a day. How long had you known her, when you made this plan?"

"I'd known her for half an hour," replied Winterbourne.

"Good heavens! She's arranging to go out with a gentleman that she's only just met. Miss Miller must be a dreadful[42] girl! Frederick, you must stay away from young American girls like Daisy Miller. You don't understand them. You've lived in Switzerland for too long. You'll probably make a big mistake. You're too innocent."

"My dear aunt, I'm not innocent," said Winterbourne, smiling. Then he said, in a serious voice, "Will you not meet Miss Miller?"

"No, I'm sorry, Frederick. I won't. If Miss Miller is going to the Château de Chillon with you, I cannot meet her. She's only just met you. She shouldn't spend time with a man that she's only known for half an hour. I'm an old woman, but I'm not too old to be shocked!"

"But young girls in America do things like that, don't they?" asked Winterbourne.

Mrs Costello looked quickly at her nephew. "My granddaughters would *never* do things like that!"

Winterbourne felt that he understood Miss Miller a little better now. His friends in America had told him that Mrs Costello's granddaughters were "terrible flirts". But his aunt said that they would never behave like Daisy Miller. So maybe polite people would always disapprove of Daisy Miller's behavior. Winterbourne felt angry with himself. Why could *he* not understand her true character himself? He wanted to see her again very much.

Although Winterbourne wanted to see Daisy again, he did not know what to say to her. He had promised to introduce her to Mrs Costello. But now his aunt would not meet her. However, he soon found out that Daisy Miller was not afraid of the truth.

He found her in the garden later that evening. She was walking about, holding a large fan[43]. She was very pleased to see him.

"This has been the longest evening ever!" she said.

"Have you been all alone?" Winterbourne asked.

"No, I've been walking round with Mother," Daisy replied. "She's gone to look for Randolph. She wants him to go to bed, but he hates going to bed. She's going to ask Eugenio to talk to him. But Randolph isn't afraid of Eugenio. I don't think that my brother will go to bed before eleven."

They walked together along the garden paths. The stars shone brightly in the dark sky.

"I've heard a lot about your aunt," said Daisy. "Mrs Costello is very quiet, and very correct. She doesn't speak to anybody, and she always has dinner in her rooms. Every two days, she has a headache. I think that that is a wonderful description! I want to meet her. I know that I'll like her. I'm sure that she's very special. I like special ladies. I want to be special myself. Well, Mother and I are special. We don't speak to everyone—or they don't speak to us. Anyway, when can I meet your aunt?"

Winterbourne was embarrassed.

"She'd be very pleased to meet you," he said, "but I'm afraid that it is difficult. It's difficult because of her headaches."

She was walking about, holding a large fan.

Daisy looked at him. "But surely she doesn't have a headache *every* day?" she said.

Winterbourne could not think of a reply. After a moment, he said, "She tells me that she does."

Daisy stopped and looked carefully at Winterbourne. She was opening and closing her fan. "Your aunt doesn't want to meet me!" she said suddenly. "Why don't you tell the truth? You don't have to be afraid. I'm not afraid!" She laughed.

Winterbourne thought that Daisy's voice trembled[44] a little.

"She's upset," he thought. He felt sorry for Daisy, and he was surprised and embarrassed.

"Miss Miller," he said, "my aunt doesn't meet *anybody*. She's always too ill."

Daisy walked away from him, still laughing. "You don't have to be afraid," she said again. "Why should Mrs Costello want to meet *me*?" She looked out across the lake.

"Is she very upset?" Winterbourne asked himself. He almost hoped that she was. He wanted to speak kindly to Daisy and make her feel better.

"I'll tell her that my aunt is proud and rude," he thought. "I'll say that we must forget about her."

But at that moment, Daisy suddenly said, "Oh, look! Here's Mother!"

Winterbourne saw a lady walking slowly toward them. Suddenly the lady stopped and moved toward the edge of the garden.

"Maybe your mother hasn't seen you," he said.

"Oh yes, she's seen me," Daisy replied. "But she won't come here because I'm with you."

"I'd better leave," said Winterbourne.

"Oh no!" said Daisy.

"I'm afraid that your mother has seen me walking with you and she doesn't approve," said Winterbourne.

Daisy looked at him. "Oh, she isn't worried about *me*," she said. "She's worried about you—or worried about herself, or something. Mother doesn't like any of my gentlemen friends. But I always introduce them."

Mrs Miller was looking out across the lake.

"Mother!" called Daisy, and Mrs Miller turned around.

Daisy introduced him very politely. Mrs Costello was right. Daisy was common. But she did things in a special and very attractive way.

Mrs Miller was a thin lady with a small nose and a large forehead[45]. Her hair was frizzled—it was dry and curly, as if it had got too hot. Like Daisy, Mrs Miller wore beautiful clothes. And she had very large diamond earrings in her ears. She did not look at Winterbourne.

"Has Randolph gone to bed?" asked Daisy.

"No," said Mrs Miller. "I couldn't make him go."

"Randolph behaves so badly sometimes. He really does make me angry when he's badly behaved," said Daisy.

"Daisy Miller!" said Mrs Miller after a few moments. "You shouldn't talk about your own brother like that."

"Well, he *is* badly behaved, Mother," said Daisy.

"He's only nine," she replied.

"Well, he wouldn't go to castle of Chillon," said Daisy. "So I'm going there with Mr Winterbourne."

Mrs Miller said nothing. Winterbourne was sure that she probably disapproved of their plan. He thought quickly.

What could he say, so that she would let Daisy go with him?

Winterbourne bowed to Mrs Miller. "Your daughter is very kind," he said politely. "She has said that I can be her guide."

Mrs Miller looked at Daisy, who was walking away. "Will you go by train?" she asked. She spoke calmly. She certainly did not seem angry.

"By train, or by boat," said Winterbourne.

31

*Mrs Miller was a thin lady with a small nose and
a large forehead.*

"Well, of course, I don't know," said Mrs Miller. "I've never been to that castle."

"Oh, I'm sorry," said Winterbourne. He felt quite sure now that Mrs Miller was not going to stop them going to the château. In fact, she did not really seem interested. But maybe she was expecting to go with them.

"We thought that we would visit the castle," said Mrs Miller, "but we haven't been able to go there yet. Then a lady at the hotel said that we shouldn't visit castles here. She told us to wait until we are in Italy. Of course, we only want to see the most important castles. We visited several in England."

"Oh yes, there are some beautiful castles in England," said Winterbourne. "But the Château de Chillon, here on the lake, is a wonderful place to visit."

"Well, if Daisy thinks that she can manage to go there..." said Mrs Miller. She talked as if her daughter was planning something terribly difficult.

"Oh, I think that she'll enjoy it!" said Winterbourne. He felt very excited now. Was he really going to take Daisy to Chillon alone? He wanted to be sure. "You don't wish to come yourself, madam?" he asked Mrs Miller.

Daisy's mother looked at Winterbourne for a moment. Did she disapprove? She walked forward. "Maybe Daisy should go," she said simply.

So Winterbourne and Daisy were going to Chillon alone. Most mothers would never let a young girl go out alone with a gentleman. How different these people were!

"Mr Winterbourne!" said Daisy, at that moment.

"Yes, mademoiselle," he replied.

"Do you want to take me out in a boat?"

"Now?" said Winterbourne.

"Of course," she said.

"Daisy! *What* are you planning now?" said her mother.

Winterbourne was excited. "Please let her go, madam," he said. He wanted very much to take this pretty young girl onto the lake in a boat. It was a beautiful starlit night.

"I'm sure that Daisy doesn't really want to go," said Mrs Miller.

"But Mr Winterbourne wants to take me," said Daisy.

"I'll take you over to Chillon, in the starlight," said Winterbourne.

"I want Mr Winterboure to take me for a trip[46] in a boat!" Daisy said. She turned round, looked at Winterbourne, and smiled charmingly. Her bright eyes were shining and she was slowly moving her fan. She looked wonderfully pretty.

"There are a few boats tied up down there—on the shore of the lake," said Winterbourne. He pointed down some steps from the garden. "Please hold my arm, and we'll go and choose one."

"That would be lovely," said Daisy. But she did not move towards him. She just stood there, laughing.

"Can I help you, mademoiselle?" said a voice in the darkness. The guide, Eugenio, was now standing next to them.

"Oh, Eugenio," said Daisy, "I'm going for a trip in a boat!"

Eugenio bowed. "*Now*, mademoiselle?" he said. "It's eleven o'clock. It's late."

"I'm going with Mr Winterbourne. We're going immediately," said Daisy.

"She *can't* go," Mrs Miller told the guide. "Please tell her."

"Mademoiselle, I don't think that you should go in the boat," said Eugenio.

"I wish that Daisy was less friendly with her guide," thought Winterbourne. But he said nothing.

"You don't think that it's correct behavior!" said Daisy, looking at the guide. Then she turned to Winterbourne. "Eugenio doesn't think that anything is correct!" she said.

"Does mademoiselle want to go alone?" Eugenio asked Mrs Miller.

"No," said Mrs Miller. She turned toward Winterbourne. "She wants to go with this gentleman."

Eugenio looked at Winterbourne, and Winterbourne thought that he gave a small smile.

Then the guide bowed. "As mademoiselle wishes!" he said.

"Oh, I wanted you to make a *fuss*[47]," said Daisy. "I don't want to go now."

"*I'll* make a fuss if you don't go," said Winterbourne.

"That's all I want—a little fuss!" Daisy started to laugh again.

"Mr Randolph has gone to bed," said Eugenio coldly.

"Oh Daisy, now we can go inside," said Mrs Miller.

Daisy turned away from Winterbourne. She was smiling and moving her fan.

"Good night," she said. "I hope that you're disappointed, or angry, or something!"

"I'm confused[48]," Winterbourne replied.

"Well, I hope that you're not too confused," she said. "I hope that you can sleep tonight."

Winterbourne watched Daisy walk away with her mother and Eugenio. He certainly *was* confused. He stayed by the lake for a long time and thought about the pretty young girl. He did not understand Daisy Miller at all. She surprised him because she was so forward. But most of the time, he never knew if she was speaking seriously. He was only sure about one thing. He wanted to take her on a trip very much.

3

The Château de Chillon

Two days later, Winterbourne took Daisy to the Château de Chillon. He had suggested driving to Chillon. He was going to take the young woman along the shore of the lake in a carriage. But Daisy wanted to go to the château by boat.

"The air is so lovely and cool on the water," she said. "And you see so many people."

Winterbourne was very excited about going to Chillon with Daisy. He felt as if he was having an adventure.

As they stood on the boat, Winterbourne looked at Daisy's face.

"She doesn't seem to feel the same way as I do," he thought. "She's very lively, happy and charming. But she doesn't seem excited or nervous."

Daisy did not look away when Winterbourne looked at her. Many other people looked at her, too, because she was so pretty. However, she did not look away when *they* looked at her, either.

Winterbourne was surprised and a little disappointed. He had expected Daisy to have the same feelings as him. He had expected *her* to feel as if she was having an adventure. But she seemed very calm.

Winterbourne liked being with such a pretty young woman. He felt very pleased that Daisy was behaving so correctly.

"I thought that she might talk too loudly, or laugh too much," he said to himself. "I thought that she might want to move around on the boat too much. But she's just charming."

Daisy talked and talked. Winterbourne smiled as he

As they stood on the boat, Winterbourne looked at Daisy's face.

watched her face. His aunt had said that Daisy Miller was common, and he had agreed. But now, Winterbourne was not sure. Was she really common?

Daisy talked about the things that they could see from the boat. But sometimes she spoke to Winterbourne about more personal things.

"Good heavens, why are you so serious?" she suddenly asked, looking straight into Winterbourne's eyes.

"Am I serious?" he asked. "I thought that I was smiling."

"You look as if you're taking me to a funeral[49]," said Daisy.

"I've never been happier in my life," said Winterbourne quietly.

Daisy looked at him and then laughed suddenly. "I like it when you say things like that!" she said. "You're funny!"

It was only a short journey to Chillon, and they soon arrived at the château. There were no other visitors in the castle, and Winterbourne spoke to the man who looked after it.

"We'd like to look at the castle alone," he said. He gave the man some money. "We want to walk around the castle slowly, stopping when we want."

The man bowed and left them. Daisy enjoyed looking around the large rooms and going up the narrow stairs into the towers. She listened carefully as Winterbourne told her all about the castle. But he saw that Daisy was not really very interested. She was more interested in Winterbourne himself. She asked him lots of questions. She asked him about his family. She asked what things he liked and how he spent his time. She wanted to know about all the things that he had done before she met him. And she asked what he planned to do in the future. She told him all about herself.

"You know so many things," she said to Winterbourne, as he told her more about the history of the castle. "I never met a man who knew so much! I wish that you would come with

38

us to Italy and travel with us. We would learn so many things. You could teach Randolph. Will you come and teach Randolph?"

"I'd like to teach Randolph very much," said Winterbourne. "But, unfortunately, I've many things to do in Geneva."

"Things to do?" said Daisy. "What do you mean? You're not in business—you don't work."

"No, I'm not in business," replied Winterbourne. "But I must do several things in Geneva. I'll have to go back there tomorrow, or the day after."

"Oh, no! I don't believe it!" said Daisy. She started to talk about something else. But suddenly, a few moments later, she said again, "Are you really going back to Geneva?"

"I'm sorry. Yes, I am."

"Well, Mr Winterbourne," said Daisy. "I think that you're horrid—you're not nice at all!"

"Oh, don't say such dreadful things," said Winterbourne.

"Yes, you really are horrid," she repeated. "Maybe I'll just leave you here and go straight back to the hotel alone."

Winterbourne did not know what to say. No young lady had ever been so upset because he was going away. Daisy was no longer interested in the castle or the beautiful lake. Again and again, she told Winterbourne that he was very unkind because he was going back to Geneva so soon.

It was now late and the sun was going down.

"I think that you're hurrying back to Geneva to see a lady," she said. "You have a lady friend there."

"I'm not going to see a lady!" laughed Winterbourne. "Why do you think that I have a lady friend in Geneva?"

Miss Daisy Miller had guessed that Winterbourne was going to see a lady in Geneva! But he did not know how she had guessed this.

"Daisy Miller is such an unusual young woman," he

39

thought. "She's common, but she's also very innocent."

Daisy went on teasing[50] Winterbourne. "Doesn't your lady friend let you go away for more than three days?" she said, laughing. "Doesn't she give you a vacation in the summer? Maybe, if you stay another day, she'll come in a boat to get you!"

While they were on the boat going to Chillon, Winterbourne had wanted Daisy to be excited about their trip. He had also wanted her to show that she was interested in him. But he had been disappointed. Now, suddenly, she seemed to be very interested in him.

"I'll only stop teasing you," she said, "if you come to Rome in the winter. Will you promise to come?"

"I can easily promise that," replied Winterbourne. "My aunt is staying in Rome this winter. She's already asked me to visit her there."

"I don't want you to come for your aunt," said Daisy. "I want you to come for me."

"I promise that I'll come," said Winterbourne.

After this, Daisy stopped teasing him, and was very quiet.

As Winterbourne and Daisy drove back to Vevey in a carriage, the sun was setting.

That evening, Winterbourne went to see his aunt.

"I visited the Château de Chillon today, with Miss Daisy Miller," he told her.

"The American girl?" she asked. "The one who has the guide?"

"Yes," replied Winterbourne. "The guide did not come to Chillon with us."

"She went with you, alone?" asked Mrs Costello.

"All alone," he said.

Mrs Costello was shocked. "Frederick!" she cried. "I can't believe that you wanted me to meet that girl!"

The next day, Winterbourne returned to Geneva.

4

Rome

In the winter, Mrs Costello went to stay in Rome. At the beginning of January, Winterbourne received a letter from her.

The Millers—those people that you liked so much at Vevey— are here. They are with their guide, she wrote. *The young lady is very friendly with some rather common Italians. She goes everywhere with them, and people do not approve of her behavior.*

Frederick, when are you coming to visit me here?

A few weeks later, Winterbourne traveled to Rome. When he arrived there, he went to see his aunt.

"Are you going to visit that dreadful Miller girl while you're in Rome?" asked Mrs Costello. "Do you still want to know her, after everything that she's done?"

"What *has* she done?" Winterbourne replied.

"She goes out, alone, with Italians," said Mrs Costello. "One of them believes that he's a gentleman. She brings him to parties. He has a mustache[51]."

"Doesn't Daisy's mother go out with her?" Winterbourne asked.

"No," said Mrs Costello. "She goes out alone. She and her mother really are dreadful people."

Winterbourne thought for a moment. "No, my dear aunt. The Millers don't know how to behave correctly. But I'm sure that they're not bad. I think that they're very innocent people."

"Well, I don't like them," said Mrs Costello.

Winterbourne was disappointed when he heard about the gentleman with the mustache. He had thought about Miss Miller a lot.

"I wanted her to think about *me*," he said to himself. "But now I know that she has met a lot of young gentlemen in Rome. She's not thinking about me at all."

So Winterbourne did not visit Daisy immediately. He went to visit an American lady named Mrs Walker.

Mrs Walker had spent several winters in Geneva, and her children attended school there. She was a very clever woman—she played the piano beautifully and painted very well. Mrs Walker lived in the Via Gregoriana, a lovely old street in the center of Rome.

When Winterbourne arrived at her house, Mrs Walker was in her drawing room[52]. She asked the servant to bring some tea. But after just a few minutes, the servant came back into the room again.

"Mrs Miller is here, madam!" she said.

A moment later, Randolph Miller came into the room, followed by his sister and his mother. Randolph saw Winterbourne and stopped in the middle of the room.

"I know you!" he said.

"I'm sure that you know many things!" said Winterbourne, laughing and shaking Randolph's hand.

Daisy was greeting Mrs Walker politely, but she heard Winterbourne's voice and quickly looked across at him. "Mr Winterbourne!" she said.

"I told you that I would come to Rome," said Winterbourne, smiling at her.

"I didn't believe you," said Daisy.

Winterbourne laughed. "Well, here I am!"

"Why haven't you come to visit me?" asked Daisy.

"I only arrived yesterday," he said.

"I don't believe that," Daisy replied.

Daisy continued talking with Mrs Walker, and Winterbourne turned to Daisy's mother.

"Do you like Rome, Mrs Miller?" he asked.

"I'm afraid that I'm a little disappointed," replied Daisy's mother. "We had heard so much about Rome. I think that we expected something very different."

"After you've been in Rome for a few weeks, I'm sure that you'll like it very much," said Winterbourne. "Is your daughter enjoying herself here?"

"Oh, yes. Daisy is having a wonderful time," replied Mrs Miller. "She goes to lots of parties and dinners, and she has made many new friends. The people here have been very kind to her. And she knows a lot of gentlemen. Of course, it's much nicer for a young lady if she knows lots of gentlemen."

Suddenly Daisy turned to Winterbourne. "I've been telling Mrs Walker that you were very unkind to me in Vevey!" she said loudly. "I asked you to stay in Vevey but you went back to Geneva."

Winterbourne was upset by these words. "My dear Miss Miller," he cried, "I've come all the way to Rome, and now you are scolding[53] me!"

Winterbourne had not stopped at Bologna or Florence on his way to Rome, because he had wanted to see Daisy. He usually visited those cities when he was traveling in Italy. But he had wanted to see Daisy as soon as possible. And now she told him that he was unkind!

A friend had once told Winterbourne, "Pretty American women are the most difficult and ungrateful[54] women." Now Winterbourne knew that his friend's words were true.

Daisy turned to Mrs Walker and touched the ribbons on the lady's dress. "Mrs Walker, I want to tell you something. You know that I'm coming to your party."

"Oh, I'm pleased to hear that," said Mrs Walker.

"I have a lovely dress that I want to wear," continued Daisy.

"I'm sure that you do," replied Mrs Walker.

"But I would like to bring a friend to the party. May I

bring someone with me?" asked Daisy. "He is my very good friend. His name is Mr Giovanelli." It was unusual for a young lady to invite a friend to someone else's party. And it was *very* unusual for a young lady to invite a gentleman. But Daisy did not seem worried or embarrassed. Her voice was clear and strong, and her face was bright.

Mrs Walker was silent for a moment, and then she looked quickly at Winterbourne. "I'll be pleased to meet Mr Giovanelli," she said.

"He's an Italian," said Daisy. "He's the most handsome man in the world—except for Mr Winterbourne! Mr Giovanelli knows lots of Italians, but he would like to meet some Americans. He likes Americans very much. Mr Giovanelli is terribly clever and absolutely lovely!"

Mrs Miller stood up. "We must go back to the hotel," she said.

"I'm not going back to the hotel, Mother," said Daisy. "I'm going to take a walk."

"She's going to walk with Mr Giovanelli," said Randolph.

"I'm going to the Pincio[55]," said Daisy, smiling.

"Are you going alone, my dear?" said Mrs Walker. "It's late in the afternoon. I don't think that it's safe to go out alone at this time."

It was now the busiest time of the day. The streets of Rome were crowded with people and carriages.

"No, it isn't safe," agreed Mrs Miller. "There will be too many people. You'll get Roman fever[56]."

Daisy stood up and kissed Mrs Walker.

"Mrs Walker, you worry about me too much," she said. "I'm not going to the Pincio alone. I'm going to meet a friend."

"Your friend cannot keep you safe from the fever," said Mrs Miller.

"Are you going to meet Mr Giovanelli?" asked Mrs Walker.

Winterbourne watched Daisy. She was smiling and touching the ribbons on her hat. Then she looked at Winterbourne and said, "Yes, I'm going to meet Mr Giovanelli—beautiful Mr Giovanelli."

"My dear Miss Miller," said Mrs Walker, holding Daisy's hand. "Please don't walk to the Pincio to meet a beautiful Italian now."

"Good heavens," said Daisy. "I don't want to behave incorrectly. What can I do?" She looked at Winterbourne again. "I know—I have an idea. The Pincio is not far away. Maybe Mr Winterbourne will walk with me."

"Of course," said Winterbourne politely. "I'll be happy to walk with you."

Daisy and Winterbourne said goodbye to Mrs Walker, and went out into the street. Outside the house, Mrs Miller's carriage was waiting, and Eugenio was sitting in the back of it.

"Goodbye, Eugenio!" called Daisy happily. "I'm going to take a walk."

The Via Gregoriana was quite close to the Pincio. However, many minutes passed before Winterbourne and Daisy Miller reached the lovely gardens. It was a beautiful day, and the streets were crowded. A great many people were slowly walking about. Others were driving in their carriages. Winterbourne enjoyed walking with Miss Miller. He was pleased that they did not reach the gardens quickly. But he also knew that it was unusual for a gentleman to walk alone with a young, unmarried lady. And Daisy Miller was a very pretty young lady.

While they were walking along, many people looked at Daisy Miller's pretty face and figure.

"She would have felt very uncomfortable if she had walked to the Pincio alone!" Winterbourne said to himself.

He felt angry and pleased at the same time. He was angry

because Daisy had arranged to meet another man. But he was also pleased that she had asked *him* to walk to the Pincio with her.

"I'll not let her be alone with this man, Giovanelli," he thought. "I'll stay with her."

"Why didn't you come to see me earlier?" asked Daisy suddenly. "You told me that you would visit me in Rome."

"I've only just arrived in the city," replied Winterbourne. "I came by train."

"The train arrived yesterday," said Daisy. "You must have stayed on the train for a long time after it stopped!" She laughed. "You had time to go and visit Mrs Walker!"

"Mrs Walker and I are old friends," said Winterbourne. "I knew her—"

"You knew her at Geneva," said Daisy. "Mrs Walker told me. Well, you knew *me* at Vevey. So you should have come to see *me*."

Soon, Daisy stopped scolding Winterbourne. She started talking quickly about lots of things that were not important.

"We have wonderful rooms at our hotel," she said. "Eugenio tells us that we have the best rooms in Rome. We're going to stay here all winter, if we don't die of Roman fever! And if we die of the fever, we'll have to stay here anyway! Rome is much nicer than I expected. I expected the city to be too quiet. But I'm really enjoying myself. I know so many people, and they're all charming. The society is very good. There are all kinds of people—English, and Germans, and Italians. I think that I like the English best. I like the way that they talk. But there are some charming Americans. There is a party, or a dinner, or something, every day. There's not much dancing, but there's always plenty of conversation. And I've always liked good conversations."

Winterbourne and Daisy arrived at the gate of the Pincio.

"Where is Mr Giovanelli?" said Daisy. "Let's look over

there." She pointed across to a low wall at the front of the gardens. People were standing by the wall, looking out at the view.

"I certainly won't help you to find Mr Giovanelli," said Winterbourne.

"Then I'll find him without you," replied Daisy.

"I won't let you leave me!" cried Winterbourne.

Daisy laughed. "Why not?" she said. "Are you afraid that you'll get lost?" She looked around the gardens. "Oh, look, there's Giovanelli! He's leaning on that tree. He's watching the women in the carriages. Doesn't he look wonderful?"

Winterbourne looked to where Daisy was pointing. Giovanelli's back was against a large pine tree. He was a small man, with a very handsome face. His arms were folded, and he was holding a walking stick in one hand. Giovanelli wore a monocle[57] in one eye, and he had a black mustache. There was a large flower fastened to the collar of his coat.

"He is *not* a real gentleman,' Winterbourne thought. "He's trying to look like a gentleman. But I know that he isn't."

"Are you really going to speak to that man?" he asked Daisy.

"Of course I'm going to speak to him," she replied.

"Then I'm going to stay with you," said Winterbourne coldly.

Daisy looked at him. The expression in her charming face was calm. "I don't like the way that you say that," she said.

"I'm sorry if I spoke in the wrong way," Winterbourne replied. "But I think that this is wrong. I wanted you to know that."

Daisy's eyes were prettier than ever. "If a gentleman tells me what to do, I won't listen. And no gentleman will stop me doing something. I do what I wish."

"Well," said Winterbourne slowly, "this is what *I* think. You should sometimes listen to a gentleman. But you should listen to the right gentleman."

Giovanelli's back was against a large pine tree. He was a small man, with a very handsome face.

Daisy started to laugh. "I listen to gentlemen all the time!" she said. "Do you think that Mr Giovanelli is the right gentleman?"

Giovanelli had seen Daisy and Winterbourne walking toward him. He stepped forward quickly and bowed. He had a wide smile, and he looked intelligent. But Winterbourne whispered quietly to Daisy, "No, he's not the right one."

Daisy politely introduced Giovanelli to Winterbourne. Then she walked slowly along the road beside the Pincio. Giovanelli walked on Daisy's left side, and Winterbourne walked on her right side. Giovanelli spoke English very well.

Later, Winterbourne found out that Giovanelli spent a lot of time talking to rich young American ladies.

Giovanelli talked happily to Daisy. He behaved just like a real gentleman. He had expected to spend the afternoon alone with Daisy. But he did not seem angry that Winterbourne had come too.

"Giovanelli wants to please Daisy," thought Winterbourne. "I can see that. He must be very interested in her. That is why he doesn't show his true feelings."

Giovanelli certainly knew how to behave correctly. He talked and laughed and was very pleasant.

"He's very clever," Winterbourne thought. "He behaves like a gentleman. But he's certainly not a real gentleman. Maybe he's a music teacher, or a very bad artist, or a writer. But Daisy can't see that Giovanelli isn't a gentleman. She hasn't learned about good manners and correct behavior. She's never met the right people in society, so she doesn't know what a real gentleman is like. Giovanelli is only trying to be a gentleman! And she doesn't know that. She is quite innocent. She's not experienced in the ways of the world."

But was Daisy innocent? Winterbourne was still not sure. Good, innocent girls did not behave like Daisy Miller. They did not arrange to meet men like Giovanelli. Daisy was not meeting him at night, it was the middle of the afternoon. And she had not met him secretly, they were in a crowded place. But her behavior was not correct.

"Daisy doesn't seem upset that I've stayed with her and Giovanelli," thought Winterbourne. "Maybe she doesn't want me to leave." He felt confused and worried. He still did not understand Daisy Miller. She certainly was not a perfect young lady. If Daisy had asked Winterbourne to leave, then he would have known the truth about her. He would have felt sure that she was not a nice girl. And he would have stopped thinking about her. That would have been easier. But Daisy was polite and charming. She talked pleasantly to both men. And so once again, Winterbourne felt confused about Daisy. She was bold and she flirted. But Winterbourne also thought that maybe she was innocent.

Suddenly a carriage stopped near to them. Mrs Walker was sitting in the carriage and she waved her hand at Winterbourne. She wanted him to go and talk to her. When Daisy saw Mrs Walker, she nodded her head and smiled. Then she walked on with Giovanelli.

Winterbourne hurried over to the carriage. Mrs Walker had a worried expression on her face.

"This is dreadful," she said to Winterbourne. "That girl must *not* do this. She must not walk here with you two men. It is not correct behavior. Several people have seen her. They are shocked."

"I don't think that you should make a fuss about it," said Winterbourne.

"She's ruining her reputation[58]!" cried Mrs Walker. "You must not let this happen."

"She's very charming and innocent," said Winterbourne.

"She's very crazy[59]!" cried Mrs Walker. "And her mother doesn't control her at all. After everyone had left my home,

I couldn't stop thinking about Miss Miller. She was walking in the city with two men! If she behaves like this, no one will want to know her. People will turn away from her. She mustn't ruin her reputation! So I came here as quickly as possible. I am so pleased that I've found you!"

"And now what are you going to do?" asked Winterbourne, smiling.

"I'm going to ask Miss Miller to get into my carriage. And I'm going to drive around the city with her for half an hour. Then everyone will see that she's not completely wild. They'll see that she *does* know how to behave correctly. And then I'm going to take her safely home."

"I'm not sure that Daisy will like your idea," said Winterbourne. "But you can try."

Daisy and Giovanelli had walked a little way ahead. Winterbourne hurried up to Daisy. He told her that Mrs Walker wanted to talk to her.

"I'll be happy to talk with Mrs Walker," said Daisy. "I would like to introduce Mr Giovanelli to her." She turned and walked back to the carriage with Giovanelli at her side.

"Mrs Walker," she said. "May I introduce Mr Giovanelli."

Giovanelli bowed, and Mrs Walker nodded politely.

"Miss Miller," she said. "Please will you get in the carriage and come for a drive with me?"

"Thank you, Mrs Walker, that would be charming," said Daisy. "But walking is delightful. I'm enjoying myself." She looked at the two gentlemen with her bright eyes.

Mrs Walker leaned forward in her carriage.

"You may be enjoying yourself, my dear," she said softly to Daisy. "But we—people in society—don't walk..." she looked embarrassed. "You shouldn't walk around like this," she said quickly.

"Well, everyone should walk," said Daisy. "If I didn't walk, I would feel quite ill."

"You should walk with your mother, dear," cried Mrs Walker. She was now quite angry and upset.

"With my mother?" said Daisy. Suddenly she understood that Mrs Walker was telling her how to behave. "My mother never walks anywhere! And of course," she said, laughing, "I am more than five years old!"

"You're old enough to be more sensible," said Mrs Walker. "You're old enough to be talked about!"

Daisy looked closely at Mrs Walker and smiled. "Talked about? What do you mean?"

"Come into my carriage," said Mrs Walker, "and I'll tell you."

Daisy looked from Winterbourne to Giovanelli. The handsome Italian was touching his gloves and laughing pleasantly. Winterbourne's expression showed that he felt very uncomfortable.

"I don't think that I want to know what you mean," said Daisy. "I don't think that I would like it."

Winterbourne wished that Mrs Walker would drive away. But Mrs Walker did not like it when people did not listen to her.

"You shouldn't walk alone with these gentlemen," said Mrs Walker. "It is not correct. People will think that you're a very foolish girl. They'll believe that you don't care about correct behavior."

"Good heavens!" cried Daisy. She looked again at Giovanelli, then she turned to Winterbourne. Her face had become pink and her eyes were shining brightly. She looked extremely pretty.

"Mr Winterbourne," said Daisy. "Do you think that I should get into Mrs Walker's carriage? Do you think that people will think bad things about me if I don't?"

Winterbourne did not know what to say. But he knew that he had to tell Daisy the truth. Winterbourne knew that

"You shouldn't walk alone with these gentlemen," said Mrs Walker. "It is not correct."

it was very important to behave correctly. And he believed that Daisy was not behaving correctly now.

"I think that you should get into the carriage," he said gently.

Daisy gave a short, angry laugh. "I want to walk. If this isn't correct behavior, Mrs Walker," she said, "then I'm not a correct person. You should no longer be my friend. Goodbye. I hope that you have a nice drive." And she turned and walked away.

Giovanelli bowed to Mrs Walker and walked away with Daisy.

Mrs Walker watched Daisy walk away. There were tears in her eyes.

"Please get into the carriage, Mr Winterbourne," she said.

"I think that I should stay with Miss Miller," Winterbourne replied.

"Mr Winterbourne, please get into my carriage," Mrs Walker said coldly. "If you don't, I'm afraid that I cannot speak to you again."

Winterbourne had to do what Mrs Walker asked. He knew this. He walked quickly to Daisy and Giovanelli.

"Miss Miller, Mrs Walker is asking me to go with her," he said. "I'm afraid that I *must* go."

Winterbourne thought Daisy was going to say something rude or unkind. But she just shook his hand. Giovanelli took off his hat slowly and bowed.

Winterbourne walked back to Mrs Walker's carriage and sat down inside it. He was not pleased.

"That was not a clever thing to do," Winterbourne said, as the carriage moved along the road.

"I didn't want to be clever," answered Mrs Walker. "Miss Miller had to know the truth about what she was doing. I had to tell her."

"Well, now you have offended her," said Winterbourne.

"Miss Daisy Miller is certainly not worried about ruining her reputation," said Mrs Walker. "I'm glad that I know that now. Now *I* know how to behave toward her."

"I don't think that she wants to behave badly," said Winterbourne.

"I thought that too, at first," said Mrs Walker. "But now she has made a big mistake. She does all the wrong things. She flirts with every man that she meets. She dances all night with the same man. People visit her at eleven o'clock at night. And when visitors come to see her, her mother goes away. Young ladies mustn't behave like that in polite society. Everyone at the hotel is talking about her. Even the servants smile when a gentleman comes and asks for Miss Miller."

"Forget about the servants!" said Winterbourne angrily. "Miss Miller is just very unsophisticated. That is her only fault."

"She says all the wrong things," said Mrs Walker. "For example, this morning she scolded you because you had left Vevey so soon. How long had you known her at Vevey?"

"Two days," replied Winterbourne.

"Ah! She doesn't know you well!" said Mrs Walker. "She certainly shouldn't scold someone that she had known for only two days!"

"Mrs Walker, I believe that we worry too much," Winterbourne said. "We're always thinking about behaving correctly." He was silent for a few moments. Then he said, "Why did you ask me to drive with you?"

"I wanted to ask you something," she replied. "Please stop meeting Miss Miller. Don't flirt with her. Leave her alone."

"I'm sorry. I can't do that," said Winterbourne. "I like Miss Miller very much."

"If you like her, you should help her. You should not see her again. If Daisy Miller continues to behave in this way, her

55

reputation will be ruined."

"I won't do anything to ruin her," Winterbourne replied.

"Well, I've said what I wanted to say," said Mrs Walker. "If you wish to go and find Miss Miller, you can get out of the carriage here."

Winterbourne could see Daisy and Giovanelli together in the Pincio. In that part of the gardens, there was a beautiful view over the Villa Borghese[60].

Near the edge of the gardens, there were several seats. Daisy and Giovanelli were sitting on seats and looking at the view. Winterbourne asked the driver to stop the carriage, and he got out. Mrs Walker looked at Winterbourne for a moment, but said nothing. Then, as he took off his hat politely, she drove away.

Winterbourne looked across at Daisy and Giovanelli. They had got up from their seats and walked toward the low wall at the edge of the garden. They saw no-one and nothing else. They were thinking only about each other. When they reached the low wall, they sat down on it. At that moment, the sun shone from behind a cloud. Giovanelli took Daisy's parasol and opened it. She moved closer to him, and he held it over her head. Then Giovanelli lowered the parasol, so that Winterbourne could no longer see their faces.

Winterbourne waited for a moment, and then he started to walk. But he did not walk towards Daisy and Giovanelli. He walked towards the apartment where his aunt was staying.

Mrs Walker Turns Her Back on[61] Daisy Miller

The next day, Winterbourne went to Daisy's hotel. She was not there, and neither was Mrs Miller. The following day, Winterbourne visited again, but once more the Millers were out.

Mrs Walker's party was three days after the visit to the Pincio. Winterbourne had not seen Mrs Walker since their conversation in the carriage. Although the conversation had been difficult, Mrs Walker did invite Winterbourne to her party.

When Winterbourne arrived at Mrs Walker's house in the Via Gregoriana, Daisy Miller was not there. But a few moments later, her mother came into the room alone. Mrs Miller looked very uncomfortable. She went toward Mrs Walker, and Winterbourne went to stand near them.

"I've come alone," said Mrs Miller. "I feel very nervous. I've never been to a party alone before. I wanted to bring Randolph or Eugenio, or someone. But Daisy told me to come on my own."

"Is your daughter going to join us this evening?" asked Mrs Walker. Her voice was cold and very formal.

"Well, Daisy's all ready for the party," replied Mrs Miller. "She got dressed before dinner. But a friend came to visit her. It's that gentleman—the Italian—who she wanted to bring to the party. They started singing songs at the piano and they just won't stop. Mr Giovanelli does sing beautifully. But I'm sure that they'll arrive soon."

"I'm sorry that she has this problem," said Mrs Walker.

"Well, I don't know why she got dressed so early," said Mrs Miller. "She doesn't need to wear a special dress just to sit at the hotel with Mr Giovanelli for three hours."

Mrs Walker turned away and spoke to Winterbourne.

"This is dreadful," she said. "Daisy Miller is behaving in a terrible way. I'm sure that she's doing this because of what happened at the Pincio. I complained about her behavior there, and she didn't like it. So now she's trying to embarrass me. When she arrives, I shall not speak to her."

However, at parties, Daisy never waited for people to speak to her. When she arrived, it was after eleven o'clock. But as soon as she arrived, Daisy went straight to Mrs Walker. She gave Mrs Walker a big bunch of flowers, smiled and started to talk excitedly. Giovanelli stood beside her. Daisy's face was bright and happy. She looked lovely. Everyone stopped talking and turned and looked at her.

"Dear Mrs Walker," Daisy said. "Did you think that I wasn't coming to your party? We were at the hotel. I asked Mother to come and tell you that we would be late. This is Mr Giovanelli. I introduced him to you before. I wanted Mr Giovanelli to practise his singing before we came. You know, he sings beautifully. I want you to ask him to sing. He has a lovely voice and he knows some charming songs. We had a wonderful time at the hotel."

Daisy spoke in a loud, happy voice. As she talked, she looked around the room and touched her dress. "Is there anyone here that I know?" she asked Mrs Walker.

"I think that everyone knows *you!*" Mrs Walker replied. Then she greeted Giovanelli quickly, and turned away.

Giovanelli smiled and bowed and touched his mustache. He behaved very correctly all evening and he sang several songs very nicely. But Daisy did not seem interested at all. She did not sit near the piano. And while Giovanelli was singing, she talked loudly.

Winterbourne had not seen Daisy since the visit to the Pincio. The last time that he had seen her, she was upset and annoyed[62]. But now she spoke to him easily and pleasantly.

"I'm sorry that these rooms are small. We can't dance," she said.

"I'm not sorry that we can't dance," Winterbourne replied. "I don't dance."

"Of course you don't dance," said Daisy, smiling. "You're too serious and formal! You don't relax and have fun. I hope that you enjoyed your drive with Mrs Walker at the Pincio."

"No, I didn't enjoy it," replied Winterbourne. "I wanted to walk with you."

"Well, you went with Mrs Walker and I went with Mr Giovanelli," said Daisy. "That was much better. When Mrs Walker wanted me to get into her carriage, I was shocked. She wanted me to leave *poor* Mr Giovanelli alone in the gardens! And she thought that that was correct behavior! Good heavens, people do have crazy ideas! I couldn't leave Mr Giovanelli. That would have been so unkind. He'd been excited about our visit to the Pincio. He'd been talking about it for days."

"He shouldn't have talked about it at all," said Winterbourne. "He was not behaving correctly. He would never have asked an Italian lady to walk around the streets with him. Italian ladies do not behave like that."

"Why is it wrong to walk around the streets?" cried Daisy, looking quickly at Winterbourne. "And the Pincio is not the streets—and I'm *not* an Italian lady! I'm very pleased that I'm not an Italian lady. I think that they have dreadful lives. They have to stay at home all the time. I certainly don't want to behave like an Italian lady!"

"I'm afraid that you are behaving like a flirt!" said Winterbourne seriously.

"Of course I am!" said Daisy, looking at him again, and

smiling. "I'm a dreadful flirt! All nice girls are flirts! But maybe you're going to tell me that I'm not a nice girl."

"You're a very nice girl," said Winterbourne. "But I wish that you would flirt with me—and only me."

"Oh, Mr Winterbourne, I'd never flirt with you!" said Daisy, laughing. "You're too serious and formal."

"Well, if you won't flirt with me, please stop flirting with Mr Giovanelli. Italian men don't understand flirting."

"I thought that Italian men understood flirting very well," said Daisy.

"They understand it when older, married women flirt. They know that these women are not being serious. But they don't understand when young, unmarried women flirt. So you shouldn't go out alone with Mr Giovanelli, without your mother. Mr Giovanelli won't understand that you're flirting with him. He'll think that you mean something else."

"Well, at least Mr Giovanelli doesn't tell me what to do all the time! Mr Giovanelli is not flirting and neither am I. Good friends don't flirt. And Mr Giovanelli and I are good friends. We are intimate[63] friends."

"Ah," said Winterbourne, "if you're in love with each other, then that is different."

Daisy stood up suddenly. "Mr Giovanelli would never say anything impolite to me!" she said quickly. Her face had become red. Now, she was shocked.

Winterbourne was surprised. Before he had talked very honestly, and she had not been offended. So he had not expected her to be offended now. He looked at Daisy. He did not know what to say.

Giovanelli had finished singing. He left the piano, came over to Daisy, and bowed. "Shall we go into the other room and have some tea?" he asked.

Daisy turned to Winterbourne. She was smiling now, and he felt more confused than before. A moment earlier she

He left the piano, came over to Daisy, and bowed.

had been shocked and angry. But now she was pleasant and polite once more.

"Daisy is never annoyed or offended for a long time," thought Winterbourne. "Is it because she's so good-natured[64]? She quickly forgets that she was angry."

"Mr Giovanelli has offered me some tea," Daisy teased him. "You never offered me any tea."

"I've offered you advice," replied Winterbourne.

"I would like tea!" cried Daisy, and she walked away with Giovanelli.

Daisy and Giovanelli spent the rest of the evening sitting together in the next room. They did not see or talk to anyone else.

The party ended and Daisy went to say goodbye to Mrs Walker. Earlier, Mrs Walker had said that she would not speak to Miss Miller. Now she did what she had promised. She turned her back on Daisy.

Winterbourne was standing near the door, and he saw what happened. Daisy looked at her mother. But Mrs Miller had not seen what Mrs Walker had done. Or maybe she had not understood what had happened.

"Good night, Mrs Walker," Daisy's mother said. "We've had a wonderful evening. My daughter and I are leaving together. If Daisy *comes* to parties without me, I don't let her *leave* without me!"

Daisy's face was pale and her expression was serious. Winterbourne saw that she was shocked and confused. He had not seen her like that before. And he felt very sorry for her. He spoke quietly to Mrs Walker.

"That was very unkind," he said.

"I will *not* let that girl come into my house again," she replied.

6

Daisy Miller Goes Too Far

After Mrs Walker's party, Winterbourne visited Daisy Miller's hotel several times. She and her mother were often out. When they were at their hotel, Giovanelli was always with them. Daisy was often alone with him in their drawing room. But she was never embarrassed or annoyed when Winterbourne arrived. She talked happily with both gentlemen. And her conversation showed innocence and boldness. She never asked Winterbourne to leave. And she never made him feel uncomfortable. At first, Winterbourne was surprised by this. But he was beginning to feel that Daisy was always surprising. She never behaved in the way that he expected.

"Maybe she's not really interested in Giovanelli," thought Winterbourne. "If she were very interested, then she'd want to be alone with him."

Daisy was always very good-natured. And this made Winterbourne like her even more. He did not think that she would ever be jealous[65]. The other women that Winterbourne had been interested in were different. He had always felt that they might be jealous. He had often thought that he might be afraid of them. But when he was with Daisy he never felt nervous. He felt comfortable and happy. But Winterbourne felt that Daisy was probably a foolish young woman.

But Daisy *was* very interested in Giovanelli. She looked at him whenever he spoke. She was always telling him what to do. And she was always teasing him. Maybe she had forgotten about what had happened at Mrs Walker's party. Maybe she had forgotten that Winterbourne had shocked and upset her.

One Sunday afternoon, Winterbourne went to the great church of St Peter with his aunt. He saw Daisy and Giovanelli walking around inside the beautiful building together. After a few minutes, he told Mrs Costello that the two young people were also in St Peter's. He pointed toward them.

"Ah, so that's what you have been thinking about," his aunt said.

"I don't know what you mean," replied Winterbourne.

"You've been thinking about something since we arrived," said Mrs Costello. "Now I know what it is. You're thinking about that young lady, Miss Baker, Miss Chandler—what's her name? Ah yes, Miss *Miller*. You're thinking about her and her secret love affair with that Italian."

"I don't think that they're having an affair," replied Winterbourne, quietly.

"Everyone in Rome is talking about it," said Mrs Costello. "People say that the young lady is deeply in love with him."

"They are certainly very intimate," replied Winterbourne.

Soon, Winterbourne himself learned that people were talking about Daisy and Giovanelli. While he and his aunt were at St Peter's, several Americans came to talk to Mrs Costello. They all said that Miss Miller was really "going too far⁶⁶". Winterbourne did not like hearing people talk about Daisy in this way. However, when he came out of the church, he saw Daisy get into a carriage with Giovanelli. They drove off together through the streets of Rome.

"Our friends were right," thought Winterbourne. "Daisy Miller really is going too far." He felt very sorry for her. People were saying that she was a bad person. Winterbourne knew that Daisy was honest as well as pretty. He was upset when he heard people talk about her in that way.

One day, Winterbourne was walking in the city when he met an American friend. His friend had just visited the gallery of the Doria Palace. He talked for a moment about the beautiful paintings that he had seen there.

"And I also saw that pretty American girl—Daisy Miller," said Winterbourne's friend. "She was sitting quietly with a friend in the gallery. They looked very intimate."

"Who was her friend?" asked Winterbourne.

"It was a little Italian with a flower on his coat," the American replied. "The girl is very pretty. But maybe she doesn't come from the best society. She certainly doesn't behave as if she is from the best society."

When he heard this, Winterbourne went immediately to Miss Miller's hotel. Mrs Miller was at home alone.

"I'm sorry that Daisy isn't here to see you," she said. "She's gone out somewhere with Mr Giovanelli. She's always going somewhere with Mr Giovanelli."

"I've seen that they are very intimate," said Winterbourne.

"Oh, they behave as if they can't live without each other!" said Mrs Miller. "I think that Daisy's going to get married. I've told her many times that she's engaged."

"And what does Daisy say?"

"Oh, she says that she isn't engaged," replied Mrs Miller. "But she certainly behaves as if she's engaged. Mr Giovanelli said to me, 'If we get engaged, we'll tell you.' He made this promise to me. I'll certainly want to write and tell Mr Miller about it."

Winterbourne had wanted to speak to Mrs Miller about Daisy's behavior. He had wanted to say, "Your daughter is going too far." But Mrs Miller was a foolish woman. He did not think that she would care, or even understand. He said goodbye to her and returned to his hotel.

After this, Winterbourne did not see Daisy for a few days. She was never at home when he visited her hotel. And when he went to dinners and parties at people's homes, she was never invited. Polite society had decided that Daisy Miller had gone too far. Polite Americans did not behave like Daisy Miller. And they wanted Europeans to know that. They wanted Europeans to see that they were turning their backs on her.

"Nobody wants to be friends with Daisy Miller now," thought Winterbourne. "How does she feel about that?"

Sometimes, Winterbourne thought that Daisy did not feel anything at all. This thought annoyed him.

"Daisy is a foolish child who doesn't have good manners," he said to himself. "People have turned their backs on her, but maybe she doesn't even think about it. Maybe she hasn't seen what people in society are doing."

At other times, Winterbourne thought differently.

"Daisy understands exactly what is happening," he said to himself. "She just doesn't care. Is this because she knows that she's innocent? Or is it because she's a crazy young girl? Now I feel less sure that Daisy is innocent. But I still don't completely understand her. Why does she behave so badly? Do all young Americans behave like this today? Or is Daisy behaving like other people from her position in society? Does Daisy Miller always do exactly what she wishes?"

Winterbourne was certain about one thing. He would never become intimate with Daisy now. It was too late. She was with Giovanelli.

A few days after his meeting with Mrs Miller, Winterbourne saw Daisy again. He was visiting the ruins of the Palace of the Caesars[67]. It was a beautiful spring day, and the air smelled of flowers. Winterbourne looked across at the view of the city.

"Rome has never been as lovely as this," he thought.

Suddenly he saw Daisy. She was walking among the ruins of the palace, with Giovanelli at her side. And she looked prettier than ever. When Daisy and Giovanelli saw Winterbourne, they walked toward him.

She was walking among the ruins of the palace, with Giovanelli at her side.

"Well," said Daisy. "Aren't you lonely, Mr Winterbourne?"

"Lonely?" he said.

"You're always alone," said Daisy. "Will no-one walk with you?"

"I'm not as lucky as Mr Giovanelli," replied Winterbourne.

Giovanelli had always behaved very politely towards Winterbourne. He listened when Winterbourne was talking. He laughed pleasantly at the things Winterbourne said. And he never seemed jealous. Now he politely walked away from Daisy and Winterbourne. He picked a flower, and fastened it carefully onto the collar of his coat.

"I know why you say that," said Daisy, watching Giovanelli. "You think that I go out with Mr Giovanelli too much."

"Everyone thinks that you go out with him too much," said Winterbourne. "But do you care what other people think?"

"Yes, of course!" said Daisy seriously. "But I don't believe that people are shocked. They don't really care what I do."

"I think that they *do* care," said Winterbourne. "I think that they'll show their feelings. And it won't be pleasant."

"What do you mean?" Daisy asked.

"People will turn their backs on you," he replied. "They'll not want to be friends with you."

Daisy's face became red. "Mrs Walker turned her back on me the other night. Everyone will start to do that. Is that what you mean?" she asked.

"Yes, exactly!" replied Winterbourne.

Daisy looked at Giovanelli. He was touching the flower on his coat. She looked back at Winterbourne.

"I'm sure that people won't be so unkind. I don't think that you would let them," she said.

"I can't stop them," he replied. He was quiet for a moment. "Your mother told me that you are engaged."

"Did she?" said Daisy.

"Does Randolph believe that you're engaged?" asked Winterbourne, laughing.

"I don't think that my brother believes anything," replied Daisy, and Winterbourne laughed again. As Giovanelli walked back toward them, Daisy turned to Winterbourne.

"Well," she said, "I *am* engaged."

Winterbourne did not laugh now.

"You don't believe me!" said Daisy.

Winterbourne said nothing for a moment. "Yes, I believe you!" he said at last.

"No, you don't," replied Daisy. "Well, then, I'm *not* engaged!"

Giovanelli walked up to Daisy and held her arm. They said goodbye to Winterbourne and went away toward the gate.

Winterbourne watched them for a moment. Then he turned away and walked back toward the ruins.

7

Winterbourne Makes a Decision

A few weeks later, Winterbourne went to dinner at a house on the Caelian Hill[68]. After dinner, he decided not to go home in a carriage. He wanted to walk. It was a beautiful evening, with a pale moon shining in the dark sky.

It was about eleven o'clock when Winterbourne reached the Colosseum[69], and he decided to go inside. He wanted to see the great arena by the light of the moon.

Outside the Colosseum, a small carriage was waiting.

Winterbourne walked past it and went through one of the open doorways into the arena.

The big arena looked wonderful. Part of the building was in darkness, but pale moonlight shone on the other part of it. Winterbourne sat for a few minutes, enjoying the view. Then suddenly he stood up. He had remembered that the Colosseum was a dangerous place at night. There was illness in this part of the city. People sometimes caught Roman fever here.

Winterbourne decided to leave. He walked quickly toward the center of the arena. In the center of the Colosseum, there was a large cross on the top of some stone steps. The steps and the cross were in darkness now. As he approached the cross, Winterbourne saw two people there. A woman was sitting on the steps. And a man was standing in front of her.

"He's looking at us," said the woman's voice. "He looks like one of the wild animals that used to kill people here."

Winterbourne knew the woman's voice. She spoke with an American accent. It was Daisy Miller.

"I hope that he's not too hungry," said the man. "He'll have to kill me first. Then he can eat you!" It was Giovanelli!

Winterbourne stopped immediately. He was shocked. Why was Miss Miller alone here with Giovanelli, so late at night? But Winterbourne was also relieved. He felt that great worry had been taken away from him. At last he knew what Daisy Miller was really like. For a long time, he had been confused about her. But now he understood her behavior at last. Winterbourne did not have to be kind and polite to Daisy now. She was not a nice girl. He felt angry with himself. He had spent so much time thinking about Daisy Miller. He had not known if she was a good or a bad person. Now, at last, he knew the answer.

Daisy and Giovanelli were in the darkness, and he could

*As he approached the cross, Winterbourne saw
two people there.*

not see them clearly. He thought that they could not see him either. But he was standing in the pale moonlight. So when he turned away and started to walk back toward the doorway, Daisy and Giovanelli saw him clearly.

"It was Mr Winterbourne!" said Daisy. "He saw me—and he turned his back on me!"

Winterbourne heard what Daisy said. "She's very clever," he thought. "She's trying to show that she's offended. She wants me to think that she's innocent."

However, Winterbourne did not want to be rude. He turned around and walked back toward Daisy and Giovanelli. The moonlight was now shining on them. Daisy stood up and Giovanelli took off his hat. Daisy looked lovely in the moonlight.

"How long have you been here?" Winterbourne asked Daisy in a cold voice.

"All evening," she said. "The Colosseum is lovely in the moonlight. I've never seen anything so pretty."

"I'm afraid that Roman fever is not very pretty," said Winterbourne. He turned to Giovanelli. "You're a Roman," he said. "You know that it's dangerous to spend the evening here."

"I am not afraid," said Giovanelli.

"No," replied Winterbourne, "I'm sure that you are not afraid. But *I'm* afraid for this young lady. She could become very ill."

"I told Miss Miller that we should not come here," replied Giovanelli calmly. "But Miss Miller would not listen."

"I've never been ill, and I won't be ill now!" said Daisy. "I wanted to see the Colosseum in the moonlight. I wouldn't have gone home without seeing that. And we've had a delightful time, haven't we, Mr Giovanelli? Eugenio has some very good pills[70]. If I become ill, he'll give me some pills."

"You should drive home as fast as possible," said Winterbourne. "And you should take one of those pills."

"Mr Winterbourne is right," said Giovanelli. "I will ask the driver to get the carriage ready." And he walked away quickly.

Daisy walked toward the doorway with Winterbourne. He saw that she was not at all embarrassed. Daisy talked happily about the beauty of the arena.

"Well, I've seen the Colosseum in the moonlight," she said. "I'm very glad about that." She was quiet for a moment. "Why don't you say something?" she asked. But Winterbourne just laughed. They walked out through the doorway, and found Giovanelli waiting with the carriage.

"When I saw you at the Palace of the Caesars, I told you that I was engaged," Daisy said. "Did you believe me?"

"It doesn't matter what I believed," said Winterbourne.

"Well, what do you believe now?" Daisy asked.

"I believe that it isn't important," said Winterbourne. "I don't care if you are engaged or not!"

Daisy started to say something, but Giovanelli came up and held her arm. "Quick, quick!" he said. "We must get inside."

Daisy got into the carriage, and Giovanelli sat down beside her.

"Take some of Eugenio's pills!" said Winterbourne. "Don't forget!" And he took off his hat and bowed.

"I don't care if I get Roman fever!" said Daisy, in a strange voice. And the carriage drove away.

Winterbourne did not tell anyone that he had seen Giovanelli and Daisy at the Colosseum. But soon everyone was talking about it. Soon everyone knew that Miss Daisy Miller had stayed in the Colosseum until midnight with a gentleman.

"The servants must have talked about her behavior,"

Winterbourne thought. But he didn't feel angry. "I don't care if the servants talk about Daisy Miller now."

However, a day or two later, Winterbourne heard some dreadful news. Daisy was very ill. She had caught Roman fever. Winterbourne immediately went to her hotel. Two or three other people were already there, talking to Randolph.

"She was always going out at night," said the young boy. "That's why she's ill. I don't know why she liked going out at night. It's so dark. You can't see anything here at night. In America there's always a bright moon!"

The visitors did not see Mrs Miller. She was in her daughter's room. For too long, Mrs Miller had let Daisy do what she wanted. But now, at last, Mrs Miller was taking good care of her daughter.

Winterbourne often returned to the hotel to ask about Daisy. One day he did see Mrs Miller. She was very worried about her daughter, but she was calm.

"I always thought that Mrs Miller was a very foolish, weak woman," Winterbourne said to himself. "But maybe she's not such a bad person."

"Daisy spoke about you the other day," Mrs Miller said to Winterbourne. "A lot of the time, her fever is very bad, and she doesn't know what she's saying. But she asked me to give you this message. She never was engaged to Mr Giovanelli. I'm very glad. Mr Giovanelli hasn't been to see Daisy since she became ill. I thought that he was a real gentleman. But he has not shown polite behavior! I heard that he's afraid of me. He thinks that I'm angry because he took Daisy out at night. Well, I am angry. But I'm a lady. I would never scold him."

Mrs Miller was silent for a moment, then she went on.

"Daisy says, 'I'm not engaged. Please tell Mr Winterbourne.' She said that three times. I don't know why she wanted you to know. Oh, and she said, 'Does Mr Winterbourne remember going to that castle in Switzerland with me?'"

Winterbourne had been right. It was not important if Daisy was engaged or not. A week later, she died. The Roman fever had been very serious indeed.

Daisy's funeral took place a few days later. Quite a few people attended, although they had disapproved of Miss Miller when she was alive. Giovanelli stood near to Winterbourne.

After the funeral, Giovanelli and Winterbourne walked away together. Giovanelli's face was very pale, and there was no flower fastened to his coat. After a few moments, he said, "Miss Miller was the most beautiful and good-natured young lady that I have ever met. And she was the most innocent lady that I have ever met too."

"The most innocent?" Winterbourne repeated.

"Yes. The most innocent!" said Giovanelli.

"Why did you take her to the Colosseum?" Winterbourne asked angrily.

Giovanelli looked at the ground, and then up at Winterbourne. "I was not afraid for myself," he said. "And she wanted to go."

"Well, you were foolish!" said Winterbourne.

Giovanelli looked down again. "She would never have married me, I am sure," he said.

"She wouldn't have married you?" said Winterbourne.

"No, I am sure," Giovanelli replied softly. "At first, I hoped that she would marry me. But no, she would never have married me."

Winterbourne looked at the flowers on Daisy's grave. When he looked up again, Giovanelli had gone.

A few days after Daisy's funeral, Winterbourne left Rome. But he often thought about her. The next summer, he went again to visit his aunt, Mrs Costello, at Vevey.

"Do you remember that American girl, Daisy Miller?" he

said to his aunt one day. "I often think about her. I didn't behave well toward her."

"What happened?" asked Mrs Costello.

"I didn't believe that she was honest and innocent," said Winterbourne. "Daisy sent me a message before she died. I didn't understand her words then. But I understand them now. She wanted me to like her, and believe her."

"You always liked that girl," said his aunt. "She wanted to fall in love with you. Is that what you're saying?"

Winterbourne did not answer his aunt's question. He was quiet for a moment. At last he spoke.

"Dear aunt, last summer you said something important. You said, 'Frederick, you've lived in Switzerland for too long. You'll probably make a big mistake. You're too innocent.' You were right. I *did* make a mistake."

However, Winterbourne returned to Geneva and lived his life as before. Some people said that Frederick Winterbourne was studying hard. And other people said that he was very interested in a clever foreign lady who lived there.

Points for Understanding

1

1 What is the name of (a) the mountain (b) the castle that can be seen from the Trois Couronnes?
2 Why cannot Winterbourne see his aunt on the morning after he arrives in Vevey?
3 Describe the person who asks for sugar.
4 Why is Winterbourne not sure what to do when he meets the pretty young woman?
5 Why does Randolph want to leave Europe and go back to America?
6 "She's just a pretty American flirt." Why does Winterbourne think this?
7 Who is Eugenio and why does he disapprove of the young woman?

2

1 Why does Mrs Costello think that Daisy Miller is common?
2 Winterbourne is embarrassed when he meets Daisy in the garden in the evening. Why?
3 Give your opinion of Daisy's mother. Do you think that she shows her daughter how to behave correctly?

3

1 What are Winterbourne's feelings about Daisy, as they stand on the boat?
2 How does Daisy tease Winterbourne?
3 What promise does Daisy want Winterbourne to make?
4 Why is Mrs Costello shocked?

4

1 What does Mrs Costello tell her nephew when he arrives in Rome?
2 How does Daisy scold Winterbourne when she arrives at Mrs
    Walker's party?
3 Who is 'the most handsome man in the world'?
4 Why are these people worried about Daisy's visit to the Pincio?
    (a) Mrs Walker (b) Mrs Miller (c) Winterbourne.
5 What is Daisy's reply to Mrs Walker's invitation?
6 Who does Winterbourne see when Mrs Walker drives away? What
    happens next? And how will this ruin Daisy's reputation even
    more?

5

1 Daisy is late for Mrs Walker's party. What reason does Mrs Miller
    give?
2 What do you think about Daisy's behavior toward Mrs Walker?
    Use these words in your answer: *annoy offend correct behavior
    disapprove innocent polite society*
3 Daisy and Winterbourne have a conversation about friends and
    flirting. Why is Daisy offended?
4 What happens at the end of the party? Why?

6

1 Daisy is different from other women that Winterbourne has been
    interested in. Why?
2 "I think that they will show their feelings." Who is Winterbourne
    talking to? What do his words mean? Why has he said them?

7

1 What is the Colosseum?
2 Who does Winterbourne see there and what does he hear?
2 What happens at the end of the story to these people: (a) Daisy
   (b) Giovanelli (c) Winterbourne?

Glossary

1 **tutors** (page 4)
teachers who give private lessons.

2 **reviews** (page 4)
articles or reports about books, plays, paintings, etc. The person who writes a *review* gives their own thoughts about the book, artist or playwright, etc.

3 **county** (page 4)
The United Kingdom of Great Britain is made up of England, Scotland, Wales and Northern Ireland. These areas are divided into smaller parts called *counties*.
A *state* is a region of a country with its own government, e.g. in America, the state of New York is a region.

4 **British citizen** (page 4)
a *citizen* is someone who has been given the right to live in a country for the rest of his or her life. Henry James was born in the U.S., but he chose to live in Britain. He became a *British citizen*.

5 **admired**—*to admire* (page 5)
if you like the way that someone looks, works, or behaves, you *admire* that person. You are that person's *admirer*. The feeling that you have is *admiration*.

6 **writing career** (page 5)
a *career* is a job that you are trained to do. Henry James worked hard and became a good writer. He earned money from his writing.

7 **culture and polite society** (page 5)
the way that people behave, and their ideas and beliefs is their *culture*. *Society* is a group of people who live in a similar way and like the same things. *The polite society* was a group of people who had money, property and power. In the nineteenth century, these people came from the highest class of society. They did not work. They enjoyed music, poetry, art and conversations. They traveled to see unusual places and interesting things. Good manners—the correct way that people behaved and spoke—were very important. Well-educated members of polite society usually spoke quietly and intelligently. They thought about other people's feelings. They made sure that they did not upset other people. People who came from a lower class, or a poor family, could not easily become members of polite society.

8 **formal** (page 5)

official or serious. *Formal* behavior is correct behavior. Something is *informal* if it is not official or serious.

9 **psychology** (page 5)

the study of people's minds and how their minds make them behave.

10 **honor** (page 5)

a prize that is usually given to someone because they have done something brave or good. The government of Britain gave Henry James the Order of Merit because he was an extremely good writer and he had lived in Britain for many years.

11 **flirts**—*to flirt* (page 6)

behave in a way that shows your romantic or sexual feelings for a person. Someone who behaves in this way is a *flirt*.

12 **spends time**—*to spend time* (page 6)

stay somewhere or do something for a period of time.

13 **shore** (page 11)

the land that is on the edge of an ocean or lake.

14 **crowded with** (page 11)

containing a lot of people or things.

15 **crowns** (page 11)

circular decorations that kings or queens wear on their heads.

16 **fashionable** (page 11)

people who like things that are popular at a particular time. For example, clothes, music, art, etc.

17 **accents** (page 11)

your *accent*—the way that you speak—shows people which part of the world you come from. It might also show people the class of society that you come from.

18 **neatly-dressed** (page 11)

the men who work in the restaurant of the hotel dress carefully and arrange their clothes nicely.

19 **towers** (page 11)

tall and narrow parts of buildings.

20 **lumps** (page 12)

pieces of something that do not have a smooth shape. Sugar was made in one large piece. The piece was then broken into smaller *lumps*.

21 **be mad with me** (page 14)
be angry.

22 **not my fault** (page 14)
if someone has a problem, but you did nothing to make that problem, it is *not your fault*.

23 **candy** (page 14)
a sweet American food made of sugar, or chocolate.

24 **frills and ribbons** (page 15)
pretty decorations that are used on clothes. *Frills* are long pieces of cloth that have many folds in them. *Ribbons* are long, very thin pieces of colored cloth that are used to tie things together.

25 **parasol** (page 15)
a kind of umbrella that women carried in the summer to keep the sun off their faces. See the illustration on page 16.

26 **bowed**—*to bow* (page 15)
bend your head and the top part of your body toward someone when you meet them. *Bowing* was the polite way that men greeted someone in the nineteenth century.

27 **bold** (page 15)
never afraid of doing something. A person who behaves in this way shows *boldness*. Winterbourne is not sure if he should have spoken to a young woman who is alone. This is not correct behavior for a member of polite society.

28 **embarrassed**—*to be embarrassed* (page 17)
if you feel nervous, afraid, or foolish, you are *embarrassed*. The feeling that you have is *embarrassment*.

29 **expression** (page 17)
the way that your face shows your feelings. Your *expression* shows if you are happy or sad, angry or worried. It shows if you love or hate someone.

30 **honest and innocent** (page 17)
an *honest* person tells the truth and never breaks a law. A person who has no experience of the world, and no experience of sexual relationships, is *innocent*.

31 **Schenectady** (page 18)
a city in the east of the state of New York.

32 **smart** (page 19)
very clever.

33 **complaining**—*to complain* (page 19)
say that you are not happy about something or someone.

34 **charming** (page 19)
very attractive and pleasant.
35 **forward** (page 20)
Daisy tells everyone what she thinks. In particular, she speaks in this way to men. Polite society does not like this behavior.
36 **calmly** (page 21)
speak or behave quietly and gently.
37 **offended**—*to be offended* (page 21)
be upset or angry about something that someone has said or done.
38 **watch-chain** (page 22)
in the nineteenth century, a man wore a small clock on a gold or silver chain, that was fastened to a pocket of his coat.
39 **Mademoiselle** (page 22)
the French word for a young, unmarried woman.
40 **approve** (page 22)
think that someone or something is good. If you do not think that something is good, you *disapprove* of it.
41 **common** (page 26)
someone who has had little education, and speaks and behaves in a loud way is *common*.
42 **dreadful** (page 27)
very unpleasant.
43 **fan** (page 28)
a flat object that a woman held in her hand. If she became too hot, she waved the *fan* to move the air near her face.
44 **trembled**—*to tremble* (page 30)
the way that your body moves if you are cold, frightened, or afraid.
45 **forehead** (page 31)
the part of your face that is between your eyes and hair.
46 **trip** (page 34)
a short journey to see an interesting place or thing.
47 **make a fuss** (page 35)
behavior that shows you are frightened or worried about unimportant things.
48 **confused**—*to be confused* (page 35)
unable to understand something or think clearly about it.
49 **funeral** (page 38)
a ceremony that takes place after someone dies. After a *funeral*, the body of the dead person is *buried* in the ground. The place where the person's body is buried is called a *grave*.

50 **teasing**—*to tease* (page 40)

say something to a person so that they feel uncomfortable or angry. You *tease* someone because you want to have fun.

51 **mustache** (page 41)

the hair above a man's mouth.

52 **drawing room** (page 42)

a comfortable room where visitors can sit when they visit someone's house.

53 **scolding**—*to scold* (page 43)

tell someone that they have done something wrong in an angry way.

54 **difficult and ungrateful** (page 43)

a *difficult* person is someone who never seems happy with their life. A person who does not thank someone who has helped them, or been kind to them, is *ungrateful*.

55 **the Pincio** (page 44)

beautiful gardens near the Piazza del Popolo in Rome. In the nineteenth century, people enjoyed walking among the pine trees and the beautiful fountains of the *Pincio*.

56 **Roman fever** (page 44)

at this time, there were parts of Rome where mosquitoes lived in warm wet ground. These insects carried the dangerous disease, malaria, in their bodies. If mosquitoes bit their skin, people caught the disease and got a *fever*. They became very ill and their bodies became very hot. The people of Rome called this disease *Roman fever*. Mrs Miller believes that Roman fever can be passed from person to person. She is wrong.

57 **monocle** (page 47)

an eyeglass for one eye.

58 **ruining her reputation** – *to ruin a reputation* (page 50)

at this time, a woman had to behave politely, pleasantly and honestly. She could not be alone with a man who was not her husband. If an unmarried woman had a sexual relationship with a man, she was *ruined*. People thought that she was a bad person—she got a bad *reputation*. People have started to talk about Daisy and they think she will always be foolish and wild. She cannot save her reputation.

59 **crazy** (page 50)

someone who is not sensible and behaves in a wild way is crazy.

60 **Villa Borghese** (page 56)

the home of the Borghese, an important Roman family, between the sixteenth and the nineteenth centuries. The house has beautiful gardens around it.

61 **turns her back on** (page 57)

Mrs Walker *turns her back* toward Daisy and will not speak to her. In this way, she shows her feelings about the young woman to everyone in the room.

62 **annoyed** (page 59)

upset and angry about something.

63 **intimate** (page 60)

Daisy means that she and Giovanelli spend time together, talking about many things. The word is usually used about two people who love each other and have a very close relationship.

64 **good-natured** (page 62)

kind and friendly. A good-natured person is not easily annoyed.

65 **jealous** (page 63)

if someone has something that you want, or does something that you want to do, you are *jealous. Jealousy* is this feeling of sadness and anger. You might be jealous of someone because they spend time with a person who you love or like.

66 **going to far**—*to go too far* (page 64)

to behave in a way that shocks polite society.

67 **ruins of the Palace of the Caesars** (page 66)

ruins are the parts of a building that remain when most of it has been damaged. *The Palace of the Caesars* was the home of the rulers of Rome. It was built in 1 BC for Emperor Domitian. The palace stood on the Palatine Hill, near the Colosseum.

68 **Caelian Hill** (page 69)

Rome was built about 650 BC. The city was built on seven hills and a wall was built around it. One of these hills is the *Caelian Hill.*

69 **Colosseum** (page 69)

a large, very old building made of stone that stands in the center of Rome. The Colosseum was built between AD 72 and AD 80 by Vespasian and Titus Flavius, emperors of Rome. The building—called an arena—has a long, round shape. 50,000 people could sit in the seats. Games were held in the Colosseum. There were also races and battles there. Wild animals fought together. Men fought wild animals, or other men. Many Christians were also killed in the arena. At the time of this story, there was a tall cross in the center of the arena. This was to remember the Christians who had died there.

70 *pills* (page 72)
small pieces of solid medicine.

Exercises

Vocabulary: meanings of words from the story

Put the words and phrases in the box next to the correct meanings.

> disappointed   ribbons   tutor   ungrateful   gentleman
> shore   candy   frills   parasol   tease   bold   embarrass
> upset   expression   bow   smart   popular   intelligent
> society   shocked   approve   notice   common
> unsophisticated   dreadful   fan   terribly   trip   fuss
> tower   horrid   fashionable   funeral

1		good at thinking clearly and quickly and understanding difficult ideas
2		someone who gives private lessons in a subject
3		something that is popular at a particular time; in this story it refers to clothes
4		an educated man who is always polite and honest
5		liked by many people
6		the land that is on the edge of a lake, river or ocean
7		a tall, narrow structure that stands alone or is part of a castle or other large building
8		clever (this word has another meaning)
9		unhappy because something you hoped for or expected did not happen
10		people in general living together in organized communities with laws and traditions controlling the way they behave; in Daisy Miller the word means 'the better sort of people' who are rich and polite

11		very surprised and upset
12		to have a positive feeling towards someone or something that you consider to be good or suitable
13		to become conscious of someone or something by seeing, hearing, feeling, or smelling
14		usual; with no special status or rank; in Daisy Miller the word refers to ordinary people who are not educated
15		not knowing much about things such as art, literature and music that educated people like; also to know little of the ways of the world
16		very unpleasant; often used before a noun to emphasize or exaggerate how bad something is
17		a device used to move air and make it feel cooler (this word has another meaning)
18		very or extremely; often used before a noun to emphasize or exaggerate how bad something is
19		a short journey or visit when you go somewhere and come back (this word has another meaning)
20		a lot of unnecessary worry or excitement about something
21		a ceremony to bury or burn someone who has died
22		a forward movement of the top part of your body that shows respect
23		extremely unpleasant or shocking
24		to embarrass or annoy someone in order to have fun
25		not thankful to someone who has helped you

26	the American word for sweets
27	long pieces of coloured cloth or paper used for decoration
28	decorations made of narrow pieces of cloth with many folds
29	a type of umbrella used to give shade in the sun
30	confident and not afraid; in Daisy Miller it means not shy or modest
31	to make someone feel nervous, ashamed, or stupid
32	sad, worried, troubled, or ill
33	the look on someone's face that shows their thoughts or feelings; (the word has another meaning)

Writing: rewrite sentences

Rewrite the sentences using the words from the previous exercise to replace the words underlined.

Example: And she was holding <u>an umbrella to shade herself from the sun</u>.
You write: *And she was holding a parasol.*

1 The waiter took her order and <u>moved his head forward briefly</u>.

2 The people who visited Vevey wore <u>the latest and most popular</u> clothes.

3 Mrs Costello did not think that Giovanelli was <u>an educated and polite man</u>.

4 The <u>look</u> on the young lady's face was honest and innocent.

5 The little boy wanted some <u>American sweets</u>.

6 'Have I been too <u>confident and unafraid</u>?' thought Mr Winterbourne.

7 Daisy was not <u>worried or troubled</u> by Winterbourne's boldness.

8 There were a few boats on the <u>edge</u> of the lake.

9 Randolph is very <u>clever</u>.

10 Mrs Costello was <u>surprised and offended</u> by Daisy's behaviour.

11 His voice showed that he did not <u>think it was a good idea</u>.

12 Miss Miller is just very <u>inexperienced</u>.

13 Everyone <u>observed and remembered</u> Mrs Costello.

14 I want you to take me for a <u>ride</u> in a boat.

15 'Oh, I wanted you to <u>object</u>,' said Daisy.

16 Daisy went on <u>making fun of</u> Winterbourne.

17 She was wearing a white dress that was decorated with <u>strips of coloured cloth</u>.

18 I think that you're <u>not nice at all</u>!

19 A few days after Daisy's <u>burial</u>, Winterbourne left Rome.

Vocabulary: anagrams

The letters of each word are mixed up. Write the words correctly. The first one is an example.

Example: SCOOLMUSE *colosseum*	a famous Roman arena built in the year AD 80	

1	RFITL	someone who shows their romantic or sexual feelings for a person
2	TAMETINI	relating to private and personal things, and to close friends with whom you have a romantic or sexual relationship
3	SOUJALE	feeling sad or angry that someone has something that you want or can't have
4	YONDEAN	feeling angry and upset
5	SCUMAEHT	hair above a man's upper lip
6	GOLDSCIN	telling someone that they have done something wrong in an angry way
7	LOMONCE	an eyeglass for one eye
8	TUNETRAPIO	the opinion that people have about how good or bad someone or something is
9	DRAWFOR	not shy or modest (an old-fashioned meaning)
10	DENEDOFF	made to feel upset and angry because of something that someone has done

11	LETBERM	the way that your body shakes when you feel cold, frightened, or afraid
12	FEDOCSUN	unable to understand something or to think clearly about it
13	LATFU	responsibility for an accident or mistake
14	TSHONE	truthful; not deceitful
15	NILPACOM	to say that you are not happy about something
16	GRIMCHAN	attractive, pretty and pleasant
17	LAMFOR	official or serious
18	CANTCE	the way that people speak which shows where they come from
19	PLUM	a solid piece of something (sugar)
20	LEAFTUNGUR	not thankful

Grammar: syntax

Put the words into the correct order to make sentences.

> **Example:** Vevey There in are many of different kinds hotel.
> You write: *There are many different kinds of hotel in Vevey.*

1 Daisy had to promised to aunt introduce his Winterbourne.

_____

2 Millers works for friends who The someone shouldn't make with them.

_____

3 The sky shone brightly in the dark stars.

_____

4 He expected to feel her adventure as if she was having had an.

_____

5 She liked time things he asked what and how he spent his.

_____

6 She the tea some servant asked to bring.

_____

7 American Giovanelli spent a lot of talking time to rich young ladies.

_____

8 Daisy's flowers looked at Winterbourne on the grave.

_____

Vocabulary choice: words which are related in meaning

Which word is most closely related? Look at the example and circle the word which is most closely related to the word in bold.

Example:

county   national   (area)   passport   native

1	**upset**	broken	spilled	upright	worried
2	**attend**	come	bend	incline	move
3	**delightful**	wonderful	old-fashioned	shiny	traditional
4	**decide**	separate	calculate	lose	choose
5	**arena**	field	stadium	sports	games
6	**ruins**	war	money	corpse	remains
7	**scold**	illness	cold	criticize	study
8	**reputation**	opinion	responsibility	surname	title

Vocabulary: opposite meanings

Look at the example. Circle the word which is nearest to the opposite meaning.

Example:

rich   take   hold   wealthy   (poor)

1	**innocent**	honest	guilty	proud	polite
2	**dangerous**	risky	hazardous	perilous	safe
3	**pretty**	small	nice	ugly	handsome
4	**rude**	common	offensive	polite	vulgar
5	**correct**	right	wrong	sure	sound
6	**secret**	underground	closed	private	open
7	**offer**	suggest	refuse	propose	recommend
8	**serious**	solemn	official	severe	funny

Published by Macmillan Heinemann ELT
Between Towns Road, Oxford OX4 3PP
A division of Macmillan Publishers Limited
Companies and representatives throughout the world
Heinemann is the registered trademark of Pearson Education, used under licence.

ISBN 978 0 2300 3515 7
ISBN 978 1 4050 8407 9 (with CD pack)

This version of *Daisy Miller* by Henry James was retold by Rachel Bladon
for Macmillan Readers
First published 2007
Text © Macmillan Publishers Limited 2007
Design and illustration © Macmillan Publishers Limited 2007
This version first published 2007

Illustrated by Mike Lacey
Cover by Corbis/Christies Ltd

Whilst every effort has been made to trace owners of copyright material
in this book, there may have been some cases when the publishers have
been unable to contact the owners. We should be grateful to hear from
anyone who recognises copyright material and who is unacknowledged.
We shall be pleased to make the necessary amendments in future
editions of the book.

Printed in Thailand
2014   2013   2012
9   8   7   6   5

with CD pack
2014   2013   2012
10   9   8   7   6